Contours *of* Creation

Contours *of* Creation

*Learning about God, Creation,
and Ourselves in Genesis 1–3*

Aran J. E. Persaud

WIPF & STOCK · Eugene, Oregon

CONTOURS OF CREATION
Learning about God, Creation, and Ourselves in Genesis 1–3

Copyright © 2022 Aran J. E. Persaud. All rights reserved. Except for brief quotations in critical publications or reviews, no part of this book may be reproduced in any manner without prior written permission from the publisher. Write: Permissions, Wipf and Stock Publishers, 199 W. 8th Ave., Suite 3, Eugene, OR 97401.

Wipf & Stock
An Imprint of Wipf and Stock Publishers
199 W. 8th Ave., Suite 3
Eugene, OR 97401

www.wipfandstock.com

PAPERBACK ISBN: 978-1-6667-3033-3
HARDCOVER ISBN: 978-1-6667-2171-3
EBOOK ISBN: 978-1-6667-2172-0

FEBRUARY 21, 2022 11:08 AM

Scripture quotations, unless otherwise noted, are taken from the Holy Bible, English Standard Version® (ESV®), copyright © 2001 by Crossway, a publishing ministry of Good News Publishers. All rights reserved.

For Kyoungha, Sophie, Hannah, and our dear friend Jim

Contents

Preface | ix

1. Introduction | 1
2. Creation's Creator | 28
3. Ontology and Darkness | 44
4. A Poetry-Prose Hybrid | 49
5. Words that Matter | 53
6. The Glory of God | 58
7. The Certainty of God's Word | 66
8. Missing the Good God Sees in Creation | 76
9. Complete Image Bearers | 88
10. The Corruption of Humanity | 101
11. Entering into Sabbath Rest | 109
12. Some Final Thoughts | 114

Bibliography | 117

Preface

THE LARGER RATIONAL METANARRATIVE in Western culture has greatly impacted the way Christian's read the creation account and hence the Bible. In the introduction, I try to examine some of these ideas. Yet, we all have individual narratives and writing a book occurs as we travel on our particular journey in life.

My writing of this book was guided by several influences. The first was an interaction that my then eight-year-old daughter had at her school. We had never talked about evolution at home, but one day in class her teacher was talking about evolution. She asked him how he knew evolution was true. He responded that he had learned it in school. She innocently replied that not everything you learn in school is true. He didn't address her comment, but said that she didn't believe in evolution because of her parents. Yet, she had never mentioned anything about what she or her parents believed. My elder daughter had a similar experience with teachers in her classroom, although she thought it better not to ask any questions.

This book was written to help people like my daughters navigate some of the issues when facing questions about evolution and the historical reliability of the Bible. Its real purpose is to encourage readers to see the steadfastness of God's Word as a way of making sense of our lives and the world we live in. It hopes to show that the Word of God in Genesis 1–3 provides a more trustworthy explanation of reality than atheistic evolutionary theories. But the book is not a polemic per se. It hopes to explore the creation story in order to learn more about God, creation, and ourselves.

Preface

Another important influence on this book was my wife's illness. About a month after her surgery, we began a weekly Bible study on Genesis in downtown Seoul. It was a family affair and as much a part of her convalescence as the medical treatments she received, which was meaningful for our family.

I hope others will find these reflections, helpful, or if not, at least stimulate them to think about some of these matters more deeply. For if we pick up the Bible to read and at the beginning read with trepidation, then the whole of the Bible is so read. However, if we see in the biblical tradition a trustworthy and truthful guide, then we are on firm ground to allow the Scripture to shape the contours of our lives as God intended.

I would like to thank Dr. James Houston, who encouraged me at the beginning of writing this book. Some of his suggestions are hinted at in this book—the morality of love as a response to dread and fear and God loving the freedom to love (Karl Barth). Over the last twenty-five years our family has been indebted to the genuine care, encouragement, guidance, and friendship he has shown to us.

I would also like to thank the Sarang Presbyterian Church English Bible study group, many of whom were very enthusiastic students, and the Calvary Baptist Church prayer group. Many people today are struggling to adapt to the lingering effects of the COVID pandemic. They have the task of trying to navigate a new form of daily life in a post-Christian society. The same God who spoke all things into existence is the same LORD who speaks wholeness into our lives today.

Incidentally, I am writing this preface in a bygone church where a former prime minister of Canada was a congregant and had his state funeral, and where the only royal wedding in Canada occurred. Today it is a cafe and restaurant, a magnet of secular community. I hope these contours of creation will help in better understanding the creator, creation, and ourselves.

Aran Persaud
November 4, 2021

1

Introduction

A Measured Response to Natural Selection and Modern History

Skeptical Readers

THE BOOK OF GENESIS is read with much skepticism in our present time. The very first two chapters make claims about how the world we see, experience, and think about originated. Scientists offer proposals that seem to contradict any straightforward reading of this story. At best, the implication is that science is based on objective facts and Genesis is a "religious" book about faith. Science as a discipline is not alone. Many historians, archaeologists, and ancient Near Eastern (ANE) scholars are skeptical as to whether the stories in Genesis, which come in different literary forms, contain any historically "objective" facts. Ironically, many of these scholars and scientists claim their theories best describe the phenomena we see and know in our world "free" from bias. For those who read the text as a truthful and trustworthy testimony about God, creation (including humans), and his claim on creation (including humans), the result can be confusion.

To be certain, Genesis is a religious book about faith. However, critics usually mean by this that Genesis offers the religious reader warm, fuzzy feelings of encouragement regardless of whether the events that lie behind the text really happened. The idea of "faith" in this understanding is a subjective phenomenon generated by the reader. Faith is something that religious readers bring to these ancient "myths and folk stories."

This may be understating the importance of how faith has shaped the actual events and their recording in the Bible. The stories in the book of Genesis predominantly tell of people in relationship with God. When people live in response to God in love, obedience, and worship regardless of their circumstances, they are living by faith. Abel, Enoch, Noah, Abraham, and Joseph are all well-known examples. In contrast, there are other groups of people who do not acknowledge God or willfully rebel against him. Cain, Lamech, those at Sodom, those at the tower of Babel, and Potiphar's wife, to name a few, fall into this group.

The biblical story mostly follows one particular group of people, the "spiritual seed." In Genesis, we follow along as Adam and Eve are sent away from the garden of Eden. People spread out and begin to populate the world. Then we follow one man, Abraham, who, responding to God's voice, leaves Mesopotamia and travels to Canaan. We read about the lives of these biblical people with anticipation as to whether they will acknowledge God in obedience and worship or willfully reject God and go the way of the nations surrounding them. We are given all the gritty details of real people struggling to live out real belief about God in the real world. In all these stories, this faith or absence of it centers on the God who created all things and has not abandoned his creation.

At the beginning of the story God speaks and acts directly. He speaks creation into existence. He walks and talks with Adam and Eve in the garden of Eden. He speaks with the recalcitrant Cain. He has intimate fellowship with Enoch. Generations later, he judges the increasingly wicked human race by opening the

Introduction

floodgates of heaven, but only after giving instructions to Noah on how to escape the coming judgment. After the flood, he tells Noah about his covenant to never universally judge the earth in such a way again. He becomes a friend of and often talks with the Mesopotamian Abraham. God now judges on a case-by-case basis and sends his angelic messengers to root out the wickedness of Sodom and Gomorrah. But by the time we arrive at the last figure, Joseph, God has become the "unseen mover." God speaks to Joseph and Pharaoh through dreams. Pharaoh and his court of magicians cannot interpret the dreams. Joseph is able to interpret the dreams because their interpretation belongs to God alone. As a man of faith, Joseph is able to tell Pharaoh that a famine will soon come upon the land of Egypt. Remove the God of faith from the story and there is no story.

The selection of these faith-based people and events, the recording of their lives in different genres, and the gathering of these stories into the canonical Scriptures was done by people who shared in the same biblical faith. In other words, the same faith-centered perspective has been part of the process whether in the lives of the biblical people, or those who recorded stories about them, or those who collected them into the final book we call the Bible, or those who interpret these stories today. Christians who claim to read the book of Genesis as a religious text about faith are not bringing some new and subjective perspective to the text. They are really just reading the text sympathetically.

Did the "faith" perspective of those who recorded the stories make the events in the stories any less "objectively" true? My short answer is no. But perhaps a better question to ask is: how are the account of creation, the early history of the human race, and the stories of the patriarchs truthful and trustworthy? To what extent do the stories in Genesis speak about events and people who lived in the same world that we live in? Biblical faith, whether for those whom the Scriptures tell us about or ourselves, is never an abstract idea, but always centers on the reality of people living in a particular relationship to God in a real world. This faith-centered perspective is the hermeneutical link that we share with our spiritual forefathers.

Christian readings are not the only ones with particular beliefs and assumptions about the stories in Genesis. Modern scientific and historically "objective" readings bring their own assumptions to the text as well. Below, I try to point out what I believe to be some of these forces of modernity, which have crept into the church and influenced the way Christians read Genesis. I then propose a faith-based historical reading of Genesis as a means of encountering the Living God through the text.

Evolutionary Readings and Genesis: Three Reasons for Caution!

> The greater number [the younger and rising naturalists] accept the agency of natural selection; though some urge, whether with justice the future must decide, that I have greatly overrated its importance. Of the older and honoured chiefs in natural science, many unfortunately are still opposed to evolution in every form.[1]

"The older and honored chiefs in natural sciences," whom Darwin speaks of in the quote above, were not convinced by his evolutionary proposals in *On the Origin of Species* (1st ed. 1859) and *The Descent of Man* (1st ed. 1871).[2] It would be a mistake to assume that those whom Darwin deferred to as "honored chiefs" were any less capable of making sense of his data than he was or that they weren't as smart as we are. For many who haven't read his works, Darwin's theory of natural selection can seem to have been as novel a proposal as Columbus's discovery of America. However, Darwin's proposals borrowed from and built on a general body

---

1. Darwin, *Descent of Man*, 1.

2. *On the Origin of Species* was first published in 1859 and would go through six editions to finally become *The Origin of Species* in 1872. The first edition of *The Descent of Man* was published in 1871.

INTRODUCTION

of thought that had been percolating since at least the Enlightenment.[3] The French naturalist, Jean Baptiste de Lamarck had proposed a comprehensive biological theory of evolution in 1809, the same year Darwin was born.

The Enlightenment provided the ideological framework for Darwin's theories. Its proponents made sense of the world by pitting ancient paganism (classical thought) against Christian tradition in order to gain "autonomy" in a new form of paganism.[4] Perhaps the most influential way of making sense about our world that came out of the Enlightenment was articulated by the German philosopher Emanuel Kant.[5] Spurred on by David Hume's proposal that knowledge comes from our sensory experience alone (empiricism), Kant challenged existing notions about what people can know and how they can know it. Essentially, he argued that people can only know the things their minds (rationally) can actively synthesize from their sensory experiences. So, anything we cannot sense, e.g., the spiritual realm and God, must be excluded because it cannot be known. Kant's proposal placed human rationality as the absolute arbitrator of all that we can know and how we can know it. Humankind came to occupy a role that had been traditionally ascribed to God. Kant's philosophy represents the outcome of the rationalism that the Enlightenment is known for.[6]

Not everyone was convinced of the new "Godless" narrative for human origins. One example of the tension between Enlightened ideas and traditional Christian beliefs occurred in the pragmatic American South in the Scopes Monkey Trial of 1925. This was a watershed trial that challenged and overturned the Tennessee Butler Act, a law that had made it illegal to teach evolution in

---

3. He references numerous scholars whom he relies on to support his observations in both *The Origin of Species* and *The Descent of Man*.

4. So the title of Peter Gay's book *The Enlightenment, an Interpretation: The Rise of Modern Paganism*.

5. Although his family line had emigrated from Scotland a hundred years earlier.

6. Gertrude Himmelfarb, in *The Roads to Modernity: The British, French, and American Enlightenments*, suggests that in continental Europe it was pure rationalism and in the US it was a moral rationalism.

state-funded schools in the State of Tennessee, USA. Today, almost 100 years later, many don't question the assumptions of evolution and see the creation account in Genesis 1–3 as a myth-like foil to scientific findings. For them, the truth of evolution stands as a corrective to the biblical accounts. For critics of the Genesis creation story, each new fossil discovery can be seen as hammering a nail into the biblical creator's coffin.

In the last thirty-some years alone, we have moved rapidly into post-Christian societies in the West.[7] In schools the debate assumes a non-Christian world view and quickly turns to interpreting "objective" data, bones, and fossils (regardless as to how small). Fundamentally, all these proposals arise out of a Kantian closed-world system, the foundation of naturalism. Postmodernism, which is our newest way of making sense of the world, merely takes the framework of rationality and adds a personal element. Now it is my rationally generated perspective that determines one of many truths about something. However, there are at least three observations about evolutionary accounts in a Kantian closed-world system that should cause those who hold a Christian world view to question its ability to accurately explain the origins of life.

The first comes from Darwin's observation that survival of a species is the driving force for adaptive changes. In other words, survival is the driving force for changes within a species, which eventually lead to changes into different species. As many of his critics at the time pointed out, most of Darwin's observations were made on domesticated animals.[8] There was an agent involved (in this case a human) who was selectively introducing conditions to expedite changes. The way to eliminate the need for any type of external and purposeful agent, of course, is to extend the time period for change sufficiently long enough. This allows the statistical probability and chance for something to happen to seem reasonable. Darwin mentions the geological proposals of

---

7. I base this general date on the approximate time when the Lord's Prayer was removed from public schools in Canada.

8. At least in his book *The Origin of Species*. In his book *The Descent of Man* he relies more on and often refers to the "field observations" of others.

INTRODUCTION

Sir Charles Lyell as creating the necessary time conditions for his theory of natural selection.[9] Ironically, today's mathematicians and philosophers tell us that Darwin's proposals are statistically impossible at the molecular level of protein folding.[10]

Darwin was very careful not to deal with the topic of human evolution in *Origin of Species*. In an overwhelmingly Christian society, he needed to stay clear of causing any controversy that would cause the general public's prejudice against his ideas. He makes this much clear in the introduction to his later published *The Descent of Man*. When the principles of natural selection are applied to humans, though, several problems arise. One is the problem of morality. For the English-speaking world this morality was predominantly a Protestant Christian one. Darwinism allowed God to be removed as fiat creator, but the "Christianized morality" that defined the values of these societies kept insisting that God was not dead.

Darwin tried to deal with this problem by analogous argument. For example, he tried to argue that monkeys can show sympathy to other monkeys. He insisted that the difference with human empathy is a matter of degree, not kind. But his conclusions seem rather unconvincing in the context of his naturalistic framework. His argument breaks down because within his naturalistic world he must explain his observations by a cause-and-effect relationship. For physical characteristics like the colorful plumage and wattles of birds, what Darwin refers to as "secondary sexual" characteristics, this is hard enough. According to Darwin, birds and people share a similar penchant for beauty based on the evidence that women adorn themselves with plumes and gems.[11]

The quality of morality is even less quantifiable than beauty. Morality is not observed externally as a static physical characteristic

---

9. Darwin, *Origin of Species*, 75–76. Darwin, *Descent of Man*, 3–4.

10. See the video "Mathematical Challenges to Darwin's Theory of Evolution," where renown scholars Stephen Meyer, David Berlinski, and David Gelenter discuss the statistical impossibility of Darwin's theory of natural selection.

11. Darwin, *Descent of Man*, 359.

like the color of feathers. Rather, it displays itself in certain behaviors, but also exists in our thoughts, aspirations, and desires. So, it is difficult to quantify for humans, but impossible to quantify in the case of animals. The naturalism of Darwin requires the exactness of a Kantian world, but there isn't enough robust evidence to bridge the chasm that exists between animal morality and its human counterpart.

Onto the scene came Nietzsche, who offered a proposal promising to leap over the problem of morality in a single bound. By some referred to as the child of Darwin,[12] Nietzsche had shrugged off the Christian pietism of his parents (clergymen on both lines of his parents) and redefined morality with reference to the power of one's will. Goodness was what survived (power) and evil was what failed (weakness). The end doesn't only justify the means, but now defines the moral quality of the means. This was a new concept for hitherto Christian Western thought, but not unique. It had and still exists in moderated forms in other cultures. In some hierarchical societies, goodness can also be seen as a form of weakness and indiscriminate power as strength.

The result of Darwin and Nietzsche's proposals was a humanity that could be decoupled from any connection to its creator. Darwin's ideas laid the foundation that made it possible for humans to be merely physical animals. Nietzsche's ideas made it possible for humans to be social animals. The result was social Darwinism, which depicts humans differing from animal morality in degree and not in kind. In the last century, the Nazis were the poster children for where the extreme forms of this line of thought can go.

Despite Nietzsche's efforts to rationally relativize human morality and Darwin's attempts to naturalistically explain it, we have grounds to question the soundness of these ideas. Morality is

---

12. Will Durant, in *The Story of Philosophy*, says, "Nietzsche was the child of Darwin and the brother of Bismark," even though Durant notes that Nietzsche mocked evolution at times (Durant, *Story of Philosophy*, 522). Nietzsche believed there was a selective agent needed to "eugenically" breed a race of super-people. This would contrast with Darwin's ideas of a "natural" process, even though he has an agent selectively introducing changes in *The Origin of Species*.

INTRODUCTION

woven into the complexity of being human.[13] As mentioned above, it is not always quantifiable or observed. It is not just the behavioral act, but the unique human characteristic of moral judgment that questions whether humans can be deconstructed into mere animals.

A pack of rats[14] released on an island that devour the eggs and chicks of the bird population, causing that species of bird to become extinct, may not believe they are doing something wrong. However, most people would make a moral judgment and say this type of animal behavior is cruel and undesirable. According to the logic of evolutionary theories, why should people care? The rats certainly didn't. Indeed, only in 2008, with the intervention of the US Fish and Wildlife Services working with some nonprofit organizations, were the rats on this island eradicated, making way for its repopulation with certain species of birds. However, again in this instance, we have a clear example of an agent (people) creating or "stewarding" the circumstances necessary for different species of birds to once again flourish on the island. The people involved acted from a moral perspective.

In the naturalistic explanation of cause and effect, survival of the species is unable to explain satisfactorily a human morality that goes beyond only a pragmatic animal-like desire for survival. Where does such a moral stance come from? Genesis portrays humankind as being created in the image of God (Gen 1:26). Only with the creation of Adam do we see God acting intimately and communicating himself to one of his creatures. "Let us make man in our own image," he contemplates. He then breathes the "breath of life" into Adam's nostrils (Gen 2:7). Could these unique and intimate acts be the basis for a more accurate explanation of why humans have a unique moral disposition?

---

13. For Christians, the morality of love is the truest form of living the human life as God intended.

14. This was the case in the late 1700s when a Japanese ship ran aground on one of the Aleutian Islands, which hence became known as "Rat Island." Recently, since eradicating the rats, the name has been changed to Hawadax Island.

Contours of Creation

The Genesis account clearly presents creation and the behavior of its inhabitants within a moral construct because God is depicted as morally good and the original creation is depicted as reflecting his goodness. Could the rapacious and immoral pursuit of one species exterminating another in order to survive be the result of a flaw introduced into the original creation? Christians would suggest this flaw is a result of sin introduced into a pristine and good creation by Adam and Eve's disobedience. The destructive forces we see in nature describe a world in which humankind's sin has infested creation with fear.

We are left asking whether the biblical account of the origin of sin (Gen 3) and its rapid spread (Gen 4–6) is a better explanation of the war, genocide, terrorism, murder, rape and everyday acts of hatred that are borderless in our modern world. Certainly, the evil we see in our societies goes beyond any explanation of species survival. However, within a Kantian closed world the framework for asking the question does not exist. In contrast, morality, and for that matter beauty, can never be reduced to a cause-and-effect argument.

We are also right to be skeptical about the soundness of natural selection based on the intricate composition of life. Darwin himself realized that natural selection was weakened by arguments based on the complexity of organisms, the human eye being the example he acknowledges in chapter 6 of his book.[15] According to this line of thought, complexity would point to something or someone outside the closed system who created the complexity. This type of reasoning is a variation of the cosmological arguments for the existence of God, from a Christian perspective most notably associated with St. Thomas Aquinas (b. 1225). God's existence is argued for based on what we see and observe in the world, or *a posteriori*.

Philosophers and theologians differ on whether a clinching argument for the existence of God can be made from the complexity or beauty of creation alone. The apostle Paul in Romans 1–3 suggests that the sinful disposition inherent in all people prevents

---

15. Darwin, *Origin of Species*.

INTRODUCTION

them from being able to determine knowledge about the true nature of God from creation. Nevertheless, such a simple observation about the complexity of creation can make us question whether the cornerstones of evolution—length of time and statistical probability—are enough to produce such intricate complexity as found in the human eye. As mentioned above, modern molecular science seems to suggest that on statistical grounds Darwin's theory of natural selection is virtually impossible.[16]

Lastly, there is an innate curiosity in the human mind that seeks to find answers beyond the closed-world system of atheistic evolution.[17] Most people aren't satisfied with the Kantian answer, "You can't know because it lies outside the realm of your mind's capacity." In contrast, a very legitimate question to ask those who assume the big bang marked the start of creation is: what existed before the big bang? Some, such as Sir John Primrose, who worked with Stephen Hawkings on the singularity theory, try to move out of this limitation by suggesting that our universe is a continuum of black holes successively merging into one another. But this creates the problem of an *ad infinitum* argument, where an undefendable proposition must be made. For example, one must suggest there were originally seven black holes, or there were an infinite number of black holes. But are these postulations so different from assuming that there is an infinite, intelligent being, God? Neither can be proven within the exactness of a Kantian closed world. To posit there is a God with intelligence would seem to be preferable, in my opinion. Regardless, any answer that doesn't skirt the question takes us into the realm of the unknown. In this case the answer (knowledge of this unknowable state) is not as important as the process of trying to find that knowledge. The question itself is an indication that views based on a closed-world system cannot provide a satisfactory account of what we want to know about reality or how we can know it. Views based on a closed-world

---

16. "Mathematical Challenges."

17. In my opinion, the God of theistic evolution doesn't fare much better as he cannot escape the limitations imposed on him by the closed system. His hands are tied, so to speak.

system merely categorically suppress what the psalmist calls "deep [$t^e hôm$)]calling out to deep [$t^e hôm$]."[18] Does the creation account in Genesis offer a more valid and holistic alternative? This book will argue it does.

The ultimate outcome of a Darwinian world is singularity and bland unity devoid of a satisfactory explanation of morality. The diversity we see at the origin of creation is the opposite of the outcome of natural selection. In short, natural selection is unable to explain human morality and the complexity within creation and to account for our innate sense of metaphysical curiosity. We should hold a healthy suspicion to any theories of creation that cannot address these realities.

My History Looks Different from Yours

Another challenge when it comes to reading the book of Genesis is to what extent the book tells us about historical events. In other words, what is the relationship between the text and the events behind the text? The average Christian wants to know if the events in Genesis really happened. This curiosity includes the stories in the "primeval" history of Genesis 1–11, not just the patriarchal narratives of Genesis 12–50. Did God create the world in a literal six days? Are Adam and Eve real people? If Adam and Eve are the first historical couple, where did Cain and Abel's wives come from? Where did the people that Lamech was afraid of come from? Were there really ancient angelic creatures who took human wives? What about the judgment of the flood and Noah's ark? Was humankind's desire to build a tower to the heavens an accurate representation of how multilinguistic nations originated?

These types of questions really point to a fundamental difference between modern expectations of what constitutes history and how history should be told, and the way the biblical texts bear

---

18. The $t^e hôm$ ("deep") is the Hebrew word for the primordial waters that cover the formless and void earth in Gen 1:2. The $t^e hôm$ are the deep waters that burst forth during the flood in Gen 7:11. The word $t^e hôm$ is also used to describe the mystery of "deep" calling out to "deep" in Ps 42:7.

INTRODUCTION

witness to historical events. Before we proceed further, we will want to give a definition of what we mean by the term "biblical history." The online Merriam-Webster dictionary gives a general definition of "history" as "a chronological record of significant events (such as those affecting a nation or institution) often including an explanation of their causes."[19] I propose that biblical history is an author's purposeful selection and genre-sensitive recording of a chronological sequence of significant[20] events involving real people. Biblical history explains the meaning and significance of this chronological record from a faith-centered perspective.

Further, when we say the biblical texts are historical, the focus is not on determining the history of the sources, traditions, or literature that might stand behind the final form of the biblical text. Modern scholarship, working under certain assumptions, has shifted historical questions away from the final form of the text. When they look at the biblical text, they tend to focus on the process of how the text came to be and the literary rather than historical value of the final form. When we look to the Bible as a source of history, we are interested in the correlation between what actually occurred and how it is recorded in various genres in the Bible as we have it.

Part of our challenge in understanding the biblical stories as history is that we've been conditioned to understand history from a post-Enlightenment perspective. In this perspective history is viewed as an extension of the natural sciences. History occurs in a world closed to spiritual realities and so is no longer subject to the "inferior" bias of irrational tradition. It does not recognize a God who is involved in the lives and affairs of people in the world.

Ironically, modern history is portrayed as a type of "objective" description without bias. However, we are right to question how objective modern history can be. Reinhold Niebuhr noted, "The modern belief that 'scientific objectivity' may be simply extended

---

19. *Merriam-Webster*, https://www.merriam-webster.com/dictionary/history.

20. Significant not because of predetermined categories of what is significant, but because they represent what God wishes to communicate about himself, creation, and ourselves.

from the field of nature to the field of history obscures the unity of the self which acts, and is acted upon in history."[21] In other words, in a naturalistic world cut off from God, "objective" history is still recorded by a subjective observer.

When we read the biblical text through a modern "scientifically objective" framework, we can encounter an incongruity with our expectations. This uncomfortableness can lead us to assume that the stories told in Genesis are not historical. The reason is the "objectivity" espoused by the natural sciences can only categorize the apparent inconsistencies of some stories, like the appearance of Cain and Abel's wives from nowhere, as indicating that the stories of Adam and Eve and Cain and Able are untrue. Furthermore, in a purely rationalistic world the genre of myth is categorically assumed to portray make-believe people and events for all myths. Since ANE myths deal with content that is clearly make-believe, the genre of biblical myth is also assumed to be unreal and ahistorical.

Yet, to hold these beliefs about what can or cannot be historical, we would need to make some assumptions about the authors, editors, and communities that handed down the Scriptures (in our case Genesis) generation after generation and over hundreds of years.[22] One would be that the biblical authors and editors didn't see the apparent anomalies that modern people see in the text, or they didn't think these details were important, or they weren't interested in reporting and safeguarding actual events that occurred. Another is that the content of a myth cannot in any way refer to historical events. These assumptions only hold up under a "naturalist" way of seeing the world.

We must note two important differences between the biblical text as a source of history and modern sources of history. The first is that the biblical text has been understood in Christian tradition as inspired by the Holy Spirit (1 Tim 3:16). The biblical text originates from God taking the initiative to communicate knowledge

---

21. Niebuhr, *Faith and History*, loc. 248.

22. Around two thousand years ago, Philo wrote six volumes called *Questions and Answers in Genesis*, which used different approaches of interpretation to address some of these contradictions.

INTRODUCTION

of himself, ourselves, and his creative and redemptive work in the world. Consequently, tradition asserts that the biblical texts truthfully bear witness to and explain the meaning of God's deeds in this world in a trustworthy way. At the same time, it is true to say that the human authors decided to tell about people, places, and events in a way that made sense in their cultural context and represented what they valued. The Holy Spirit so guided the authors and oversaw the process that it is proper to talk about God's purpose and the author's purpose as being the same (2 Pet 1:21). For simplicity, I will talk about the author's purpose from the perspective of the human authors, who used the literary and cultural conventions of their time.

Biblical history also differs from modern versions of history in that behind the author's purpose lies a different understanding of reality. Augustine, for example, appeals to a spiritual reality to argue against the Manicheans, a group who in his words despised the Old Testament, about what appear as inconsistencies in the sequence of creation. He clarifies the apparent anomaly of there being light on day one before the planetary bodies were created on the fourth day by explaining the light as referring to angels.[23] We don't necessarily have to agree with his interpretation, but a history without the possibility of a spiritual reality—angels in this case—will look very different than one with such a reality. For Augustine, God's existence and character were taken as the fundamental reality of existence. The exact historical nature of the events behind the text could be understood from this reality.

Augustine's interpretation is a good example of how our understanding of events can change depending on how we

---

23. Augustine, *Literal Interpretation of Genesis*, 157. We should note that from the early church up through the Middle Ages and until the Reformation, allegorical and literal readings can both be found. They share a common acceptance of tradition as a guiding principle of interpretation. Augustine's method of interpretation in Genesis includes historical, allegorical, analogical, and etiological approaches. He also believed something could be told as a sequence of events, even if those events didn't actually happen. An explanation of his methodology is beyond our purposes here (*Literal Interpretation of Genesis*, 146).

perceive reality. In a world where there is a spiritual reality, God as the source of all existence suggests that history has a moral element. We are on good grounds, then, to question the truthfulness of a biblical story based on its moral proposition. From a moral perspective, there doesn't seem to be a consistent basis for assuming the story of Adam and Eve is unreal. If Adam and Eve's disobedience didn't change the reality of humankind's existence in relation to God, God's moral imperative to judge sin becomes separated from historical reality. Would God place a curse on the whole human race because of the first couple's specific sin when there was no first couple? Are we led to believe that a make-believe story is the basis for the reality of our separation from God? (Rom 5:12). There becomes no historical basis for the inherited and universal sinful disposition of all people.

Or, further, in the early stages of human history God judges humanity through a catastrophic flood because, "the LORD saw that the wickedness of man was great in the earth, and that every intention of the thoughts of his heart was only evil continually" (Gen 6:5). If the story of the flood is make-believe and God hasn't acted against sin in this manner in the past, sin becomes an existential reality rather than a historical reality. That is, the measure of the sinfulness of humankind is no longer grounded in historical events. The focus can no longer be on God's response to sin because the stories are make-believe; rather, the focus now becomes man's interpretation of his own present reality. The inner psychology of man becomes the measure of the historicity and moral truth of a story. However, the apostle Paul tells us in Romans 5 that the universal sinful disposition of all people has a historical basis and not a psychological or existential one.

The end result of disconnecting the biblical text from historical reality is an "unreal God" who has lofty ideals, but has become dislocated from the world he is supposed to have created. It is true that the stories of the fall and the flood don't need to be actual historical events to tell us about the gravity of our sinfulness. However, if Adam and Eve weren't expelled from the garden of Eden because of their disobedience, and the flood never happened,

INTRODUCTION

then the severity of sin becomes less severe than the stories lead us to believe. These stories could be interpreted to mean that God despises sin, but he has never acted in history to stem its corruptive influence. Without a historical basis, we could even conclude that he might not judge sin in the future. Yet, the historical death of Jesus on the cross tells us sin is a serious matter and forces us to reexamine our assumptions about the historical reality of these early stories.

The two views of history contrasted above—a naturalistic view of history and a tradition-based view of history—can be traced in biblical studies. Until the time of the Enlightenment the biblical text was approached by having tradition guide how the events behind the text were to be understood. Once again, traditional readings included the belief that God is real and has acted in his creation and that the biblical texts truthfully and trustworthily bear witness to and explain the meaning of those acts. Tradition saw God as the one who takes the initiative to reveal himself through the biblical texts. In traditional readings, which could be literal or allegorical, apparent anomalies in the text were often noted, but they were interpreted within the framework of tradition, as we have seen with Augustine's explanation above.

Critical readings marked a turning point in the interpretation of biblical texts. These readings arose out of the socio-intellectual climate created by the Enlightenment. They were characterized by understanding the text free from the framework of tradition. The biblical text was subjected to the same type of assumptions and analysis as any other classical text. The outcome of this Kantian rationalism was a way of knowing about things that cut off any connection to the supernatural and hence created a world where the biblical text was no longer understood as revelation. The idea of God involved in shaping history and the Holy Spirit safeguarding the recording of those deeds in Scripture was no longer something that could be known.[24] Critical analysis of the biblical texts

---

24. See Iain Provan's chapter on the "Death of Biblical History," especially pp. 20–21, in Provan et al., *Biblical History of Israel*.

occurred in the context of this ideological legacy and is known by the term "historical criticism."

Challenges to a Faith-Based Historical Reading of the Text as the Word of God

On a practical level, biblical scholars approach the question of whether the biblical stories tell us about historical events through genre. They identify the types of literature that make up Genesis—myths, genealogies, poems, narratives, a king list, dreams, and in the case of Genesis 1 a narrative-prose hybrid. Then they argue whether these genres have the capacity to describe historical events. Some are so influenced by the assumptions of the historical-critical method that they believe the stories in the earlier chapters of Genesis are ancient Near Eastern (ANE) myths that might teach us concepts about God, but have no grounding in reality. We would want to question whether dismissing the biblical genres in chapters 1–11 as ahistorical is warranted.

In biblical studies, the relationship between the Bible and similar ANE documents is known as the Bible-versus-Babel debate and has been a focus of scholars for well over two hundred years.[25] These studies have contributed much to what we know about the ANE world and the forms of literature in the Old Testament. The discovery of ANE texts like the *Adapa* creation myth, the epic of *Atrahasis*, the *Enuma Elish*, and the Sumerian flood story, which contain some thematic content similar to the biblical creation story and Noah's ark, suggests that Genesis does come to us through the cultural and literary norms of its time. However, the extent to which these ANE myths can clarify whether the events behind the biblical texts are historical is measured.

The generally held belief is that all myths are make-believe stories. This type of thinking is not just limited to higher institutes of learning. One elementary school teacher dismissed the

---

25. A good window into some of the major players over a century ago, such as the influential German theologian Fanz Delitzsch, can be found in Konig, *Latest Phase*.

INTRODUCTION

historicity of the biblical accounts to his young students with the following argument. The *Enuma Elish* is a myth. Myths are forms of literature that are unreal or make-believe. The biblical accounts of creation and the flood are ANE myths. Therefore, the biblical accounts of creation and the flood are also make-believe stories. What the teacher did not realize is that whether the events really happened or are make-believe is not determined by the form of literature, but by the content itself. The form might set up expectations on how we should interpret the content, but only because we have been conditioned by our sociocultural environment.

That a story in Genesis shares a similar literary form and some thematic content with other ANE mythic texts does not mean that the content in Genesis is mythical in the same ahistorical sense. The Genesis account can only be a similar type of ahistorical myth if its content displays the same fanciful storytelling that ahistorical myths do. The *Elohim* of creation, however, is not the same immoral, capricious tyrant as the gods in these other myths. The gods of these other creation myths resemble evil comic book characters. For example, in the creation myth *Enuma Elish* one of the higher-order gods, Marduk, kills Tiamat: "He split her like a shellfish in two parts: Half of her he set up and ceiled it as sky."[26] The content of the biblical story has no connection with this type of immoral mythology. In the Bible, God alone creates a morally good world through the power of his Word.

Genre and the author's purpose control how history is told, but a particular literary form does not *ipso facto* determine whether an event is historical (actually occurred) or not. We see an example of this in Israel's encounter with Pharaoh at the Sea of Reeds in Exodus 14 (narrative) and 15 (poetry). Both give us the same historical event in two different genres.[27] A literary form such as biblical poetry in its own way may be just as historical as biblical narrative depending on the author's intention.

According to some scholars, ANE myths were recorded in writing to support a ritual, to give authenticity or provide an

---

26. Pritchard, *Ancient Near East*, 32.
27. Grisanti, *Old Testament Poetry*, 172–77.

aetiology, or to provide justification to some tradition or custom.[28] In the Bible, the creation and other early biblical stories teach us about God and ourselves, his goodness in creating the world, and his steadfast love in redeeming us. Myths (and fables) are interesting reads, but on a practical level if they are not grounded in reality; they are limited to functioning as sources of abstract knowledge, or entertainment. They may encourage me to change my way of thinking or motivate me to be a better person. However, without God acting in history and revealing the meaning of those acts, my fundamental relationship to God remains unchanged in any meaningful way. Ahistorical myths might teach me about the character of God, but that character would be independent of any reality that I experience or know. Myths at best might challenge me to pull myself up by my bootstraps.

The cross confronts us with the truth that God's character is known primarily through his deeds and his communication of what those deeds mean. If, as we have noted, literary genre may not have been as limiting to the telling of history for ancients as it is for us moderns, then a faith-based reading sees the primeval texts as theological history. This type of history might not be written in the way moderns would want that history to be written, or even in a way that we can interpret as easily as we would other styles of historical writings. For texts to be historical, I have suggested they must be a chronological sequence of real events that are chosen for a particular purpose. The Genesis texts fall within this framework by pointing us to God's creative and redemptive work in history.

If we assume a spiritual reality where God exists, then a history written from a naturalistic viewpoint may be the less capable methodology to record history. The type of hands-on scientific precision that comes from the Enlightenment is unable to speak of spiritual realities and we would be right to question its ability to discuss history in a holistic sense. Maybe that is why the literary forms of myth and hybrid poetry are needed. The right sphere of our brains and not just the left, rational sphere is appealed to in a way that goes beyond the limitations of the pure rationalism of

28. Dalley, *Myths from Mesopotamia*, xvi.

Introduction

modern scientific viewpoints. Rather than being a poor choice, it is possible that these Old Testament forms are the only ones that could capture a complete picture of reality and hence history.

When data suggests there may be an underlying historical reality to some of these "myths," some scholars are at a loss. In her introduction to the translation of the Mesopotamian flood myth *Atrahasis*, the translator writes, "Where flood stories are found in other parts of the world, missionaries and early Christian travelers may have disseminated them; there is no reason to suppose that they are indigenous."[29] In a closed world, one has no other option but to dismiss any evidence that suggests any credibility to the truthfulness of these stories, on any grounds. A traditional interpretation would suggest that if the flood happened, it occurred in a way that is different from the natural laws of providence that operate today. But once again we bring the possibility of a different spiritual reality into the story, one that includes God and faith. In a self-constructed closed world God is excluded and consequently our ability to determine the historical events and explanation that may lie behind the mythic-type forms.

A Historical Reading

The events in the book of Genesis progress in a chronological order and so from a historical perspective. This includes the "primeval" history of Genesis 1–11. God creates in successive days: day one, the second day, the third day, etc.[30] The key point is that we are to understand creation in this diachronic sequence. No one would argue that the mystery of creation can be penetrated through our rational capacities. However, God did create the world. The Holy

---

29. Dalley, *Myths from Mesopotamia*, 8.

30. There are different understandings for what the word "day" can mean in Hebrew. It can mean a literal twenty-four-hour period, daylight, or an unspecified period of time, like in the English usage "those days." Some scholars believe that the lack of article prefixed to the Hebrew word "day" allows for the flexibility of interpreting "day." Calvin says " . . . the creation of the world was distributed over six days, for our sake, to the end that our minds might the more easily be retained in the meditation of God's works: . . . " (*Genesis*, 73).

Spirit, who was there at the beginning, bears testimony that this is how God wishes us to make sense of our world. Not in the nitty-gritty details of dinosaurs found in the Crustaceous sediment, but in the broad strokes of the expression and communication of the triune God's glory and his personal goodness and power through his Word. Questions based on our modern perspectives about science are interesting, and we might think that these questions should guide a more complete creation account. But, as I have argued above, if the universe operates on more than just a "naturalistic" principal, i.e., the universe has a moral and spiritual basis, then science alone may not have the capacity to truthfully bear witness to reality. We are given the creation account as we are meant to understand it because this account truthfully bears testimony to how God actually created everything that we see, experience, and think about.

When we move to human history, we can follow the progressive working out of the curse God pronounces at the fall. As a result of the fall, the ground becomes cursed, which will mean painful toil for Adam (Gen 3:17). Then, when Cain murders Abel, the curse progresses from the ground to the murderer Cain (Gen 4: 10). As the curse manifests itself in Cain's descendants, we see a progression in sexual licentiousness and a brashness toward violence. Humanity goes from the ideal marriage instituted by God between Adam and Eve in Genesis 1:26, to bigamy in the case of Cain's fifth-generation descendant Lamech (Gen 4:19), and then to polygamy, where the "sons of God"[31] take any women they want as their wives (Gen 6:2).

Violence also increases to the point where it becomes incalcitrantly entrenched in human hearts. Lamech far outdoes Cain as a murderer, as is seen in Lamech not seeking absolution from God, but absolving himself of his murder (Gen 4:24). The outcome of the sexual licentiousness of the Nephilim are warrior-like

---

31. There is much debate about who or what the "sons of God" are. The Nephilim were the product of the unions of the "sons of God" and the "daughters of men."

INTRODUCTION

offspring, "heroes of old" (Gen 6:4).[32] God's reflection on the complete wickedness of man's heart occurs right after the mention of the Nephilim and their offspring. God sees and then reflects on a world that has become filled with violence (Gen 6:5, 12). Progressive wickedness assumes a sequence of time to progress. This alone doesn't prove the events actually occurred, but it does tell us that from the very beginning the biblical events follow a diachronic progression.

Moses would seem to be encouraging us to see a diachronic progression from the beginning of Genesis throughout the book. First, the particular redemptive story unfolds by following people through the use of term "seed" (*zera'*). Those who passively or actively rebel against God are the carnal "seed." Those who respond to God in faith and who receive the resulting promises and blessings are the spiritual "seed." Both seeds originate from Eve, who populates the world with Cain (carnal seed) and Seth (spiritual seed). We continue to follow the progression of these lines in Genesis until the last person, Joseph.[33] The focus is primarily on the spiritual seed.

We can assume that the author wants us to hear the story as one continuous sequence of purposely chosen events. Brevard Childs in his canonical approach makes the assertion on a literary level that a common theme transcends the primeval history (Gen 1–11) and the patriarchal history (Gen 12–50).[34] What grounds do we have to suggest that Moses wanted us to read the first part of the book of Genesis as ahistorical myth and the latter part as real people and events? In my opinion, to be selective and only read the story from Abraham to Joseph as historical is a more inconsistent way to understand Genesis. Either we read the whole of Genesis as historical (pertaining to real events and people) or

---

32. Translated from the Hebrew word *gibbōr*, translated "heroes" in the NIV, and in most other versions "mighty men." The word is used in reference to David (1 Sam 16:8), but also Goliath was so called by the Philistines (1 Sam 17:51).

33. The spiritual seed finds its fulfilment in Christ and then in those who belong to Christ (Gal 3:16; 3:29; Rom 4).

34. Childs, *Introduction*, 146.

we acknowledge that we are reading the book according to our preconceived notions of how history should be told. Moses wrote the book of Genesis as a unified whole, which forms the basis for a historical understanding of the whole book of Genesis.

Explanations of the biblical story as ahistorical myth operate on the epistemological framework articulated by Emmanuel Kant, the limitations of which I have tried to explain above. If God is real and is the God revealed in the Bible, then the definition of what can be history is very different from what we have been led to believe. Can history that excludes God's reality (three-legged-chair explanations of history) be accepted as more reliable than history based on tradition? The answer of course depends on the truthfulness of the tradition. Theological history is no less historical than any other ideological history. The biblical text refers to real historical events and explains how we are to understand them.

A Faith-Based Historical Reading

Up until this point, I have been suggesting a type of socio-ideological narrative has been influencing the way that modern Christians read Genesis. Modern science and history are governed by ideological perspectives that are rooted in the Enlightenment. At best, these types of readings cannot hope to offer a holistic version of reality, nor one that is relevant to humankind's innate moral sense, nor provide satisfactory answers to questions about creation and life. Modern scholarship that operates out of a Kantian epistemology cannot consider the reality of God sustaining and working to create and direct human affairs.

In contrast, a faith-based historical reading acknowledges that, like all histories, there are ideologies or beliefs that lie behind the selection of events and people. A faith-based reading believes that in the case of the events told in Scripture they were purposefully chosen because they reveal God's creative and redemptive work in history. If we assume reality includes a spiritual dimension and derives its meaning from God's existence, these older forms of literature may be better able to explain both spiritual and

INTRODUCTION

non-spiritual realities coexisting together. As such they reveal to people a meaningful understanding about God, themselves, and their world.

We can go even further. A faith-based reading believes that God was guiding the selection of which events and people would form part of this story. He took the initiative to speak to us through these events and people recorded in Scripture. God chose to use a human author(s)—in the case of Genesis, predominantly Moses—and work through the historical process. Moses used the literary conventions of his time, although modified. However, the process was guided by the Holy Spirit, who ensured the truthfulness of the biblical documents from their initial composition until they were gathered and edited together into the canon of Scripture. The Holy Spirit's guidance of a particular author(s) in his particular historical context ensured that the book of Genesis, as indeed all Scripture, is a truthful and trustworthy witness to God's deeds in history.

Our modern expectations of how historical events should be told and recorded doesn't change this fact. In our study of Scripture, the goal is to try and determine what the meaning of God's acts in this world are and how they relate to our lives. God's purpose in revealing these particular acts is to help us enter into a loving relationship with him by understand the meaning of his love and holiness (righteous love) directed toward us and our sinful and natural tendency to turn away from him and towards ourselves.

Finally, a Christian understanding believes that the Holy Spirit also ensures that the Scriptures are understood today. God choose to reveal the meaning of his work in the events and lives of the people we see in Scripture. By approaching the text humbly in prayer, we trust the Holy Spirit will help us to understand what that meaning is. Any generation will not exhaust the meaning of the text and will have their blind spots. We are so unknowingly conditioned by our socio-intellectual environment that we would do well to balance our modern readings with precritical readings. We benefit greatly from listening to those who came before us as they share how they have heard these same stories. Then, we can better understand how we have been shaped by the ideologies of our age. Nevertheless, if we don't proceed in humility, holiness, and love, we will miss the significance of what God is saying to us today.

In this regard, all of Genesis is theological history. A faith-based commitment to the text accepts the tradition that has been handed down. The common thread throughout the whole process from composition to collection to interpretation is the Holy Spirit and the gift of faith. Like Anslem, we approach the biblical text through the perspective of "faith seeking understanding." The literature is never an end in itself, but a means of how God wants us to understand the meaning of the events and lives of the people behind the text in relation to himself (2 Tim 3:16).

Reading through the eyes of faith helps us to hear the Word as it pertains to God's acts in history. Once we disassociate the Word of God from reality, we move away from an earthly faith reading. We are left with a controlled allegory at best and at worst a man-centered ideological construct. Allegory, as Augustine realized, can be corralled by the master key of love, but we miss so much in our readings if we adapt a non-historical approach. For Adam, Eve, Cain and Abel, Lamech, Noah, spiritual-seed Enoch, and others are all presented to us as real persons. We are told about their lives and the significant events that marked their particular historical context in a way that clarifies who God is so that we may know God, even as we are known by him.

A Christian Reading of the Old Testament?

Lastly, there is a new dimension of historicity to the Old Testament implied when Jesus teaches the two on the Emmaus road "beginning with Moses [includes Genesis] and all the Prophets . . . what was said in all the Scriptures concerning himself" (Luke 24: 27). Jesus links the Law and the Prophets to the historical event of his suffering and death on the cross. From a Christian perspective, this is the central event from which all history derives its meaning.

Introduction

The text of Genesis follows the working out of God's plan from the creation of the world to the fall of humankind to the working out of the plan of redemption. Biblical history is concerned with the rule of God's Messiah, something that is expressed in anticipation by the Old Testament writers and begun-future fulfillment by the New Testament writers. History in view of the biblical story is linear, which means that God acts in this world moving all of creation, including people, towards a particular goal or point—the redemption of creation and his people from the effects of sin and final judgment on a recalcitrant world.

To understand the text of Genesis, we do best to retravel the Damascus road. If we do this humbly and prayerfully, then I imagine our hearts, like the two disciples, will also burn within us (Luke 24:32).[35] Our sinful dispositions mean our tendency is not to stand transparently before God. Moses and Isaiah knew all too well that it is a "fearful thing" thing to stand in the presence of a holy God, and yet we are given words of comfort that in Christ Jesus we can "come boldly unto the throne of grace, that we may obtain mercy, and find grace to help in time of need" (Heb 4:16 KJV).

Our Point of Departure

Our entrance into the story of Genesis is one that proceeds by faith.[36] But it is a faith that seeks to understand the meaning of God's deeds in history and what he desires to communicate about himself, creation, and humankind. The biblical texts guide us in how to understand and interpret those events as God's work in history. Every type of reading, including scientific or mythological, brings assumptions to the text. The question is: which ideological system am I going to choose, and which more accurately portrays a far-reaching understanding of reality?

---

35. Truth is never an abstract source of knowledge, but leads to a reorientation of a person's whole being—will, emotions, intellect (biblical "heart"), and body towards the triune God.

36. The course of study for this book is Gen 1–3.

2

Creation's Creator

"You are my witnesses," declares the LORD, "and my servant whom I have chosen, that you may know and believe me and understand that I am he. Before me no god was formed [*yāṣar*], nor shall there be any after me."

—Isa 43:10

Tell children that God created everything and you're likely to get the question, "Who made God?" Tell philosophers and they might suggest you ask, "What is the nature of the universe and reality?" Both questions reveal an inborn curiosity people have to know the ultimate origin of things. Both reveal a tendency for people—children in a more innocent way—to be dissatisfied with any answer that begins with an unprovable premise about God.

In contrast, the first verse of the Bible, "In the beginning God [*Elohim*] created the heavens and the earth," tells us that all things in the universe that we see, think about, and experience have a definite beginning outside of themselves. There is another dimension of reality beyond ours and God exists in that reality. God exists outside and prior to our reality and yet God has created all things that we see, know, and experience—the *heavens and the earth*.

Creation's Creator

According to Romans 1, true knowledge of God (*Elohim*) and making sense of creation are inseparably linked. Natural science might suggest that the universe can be understood through an objective set of facts, which can be sifted through for cause-effect relationships. The Scriptures tell us that the universe operates under a moral framework and was meant to reveal the true nature of God (*Elohim*), namely, his divine glory and power (Rom 1:19-20). However, a universal innate sinful disposition found in all people has damaged their ability to make this connection naturally. Lest we think this is a minor character flaw, the apostle Paul tells us that this sinful disposition expresses itself in a willful dismissal of the knowledge of God (*Elohim*), which then conveys itself through a perverted understanding of the natural order (Rom 1:18-32).

In the past, Paul tells us, people made idols in the forms of humans and animals, all perishable things, and worshipped them. God, the true respecter of individual choice, allowed people to follow through with this deliberate and immoral decision to reject proper knowledge of him. The disastrous result for the human race is given in a litany of the "what's what" of sins (Rom 1:29-30).[1] The corrupted understanding of the purpose of creation has led to people becoming less human.

Today, people disconnect creation from the creator under the guise of the natural sciences. People assume the role of arbitrator of truth in the place of God, a form of modern idolatry. Those who worshipped idols in the past and we who indirectly worship our autonomous rational capacity share the same goal—replacing the true God with another of our choosing. Both reveal a tendency to avoid transparently standing before the creator.

Consequently, the knowledge of God can never be just an objective and neutral mental exercise. If creation should speak of his glory and power, we would be confronted with the natural inward tendency we have to defame and delegitimize God—our sinful disposition. Our efforts to construe our own stories about

---

1. These types of lists are common in the biblical literature; see 1 Cor 6:9-10; Gal 5:19-21; Col 3:5. When grouped this way, the individual sins have a collective force.

creation become defense strategies to avoid standing transparently before the God who created the universe. A proper understanding of creation leads to a proper understanding of God and hence ourselves.

In this first segment of the creation story, we will explore what Moses wanted us to understand about God and creation through the use of the term *bārā'* (create). Then we will investigate who we are talking about when we speak about God (*Elohim*), including how the picture of God at creation reveals the tri-personal nature of God.

The Uniqueness of God's Creativeness

> In the beginning, God [*Elohim*] created [*bārā'*] [2] the heavens and the earth. (Gen 1:1)

What does the word *bārā'* (create) in the first segment of the creation account in Genesis 1:1—2:4 tell us about God and creation? To begin with, the English word "created" in verse 1 masks an important emphasis being made in the biblical Hebrew. The Hebrew verb here for "created" is *bārā'*. Just as English has many synonyms for *create*, such as *make*, *produce*, and *develop*, etc., Hebrew has synonyms for *bārā'*, such as *'āśāh* (make), and *yāṣar* (form). A few examples will be helpful. In concluding the first part of the creation story and transitioning into the second (Gen 2:4), Moses will say, "the LORD God made [*'āśāh*][3] the earth and the heavens." As the story progresses to the garden of Eden, we read that the LORD God "formed [*yāṣar*] the man of dust from the

---

2. The diacritical marks (the symbols above and below the words) represent the Hebrew consonants and vowels that are behind these words. For those unfamiliar with these marks, there is not always an exact correspondence to the English pronunciation. For example, the *ṣ* in the word *yāṣar* represents the Hebrew letter *tsadeh* and has a "ts" sound as in "le*ts*." For practical purposes, the diacritical marks can be ignored and the consonants and vowels pronounced as they are.

3. The Hebrew infinitive form of the verb *'āśāh*.

ground" (Gen 2:7).[4] While the verb ʿāśāh can be used with God or people as the subject, and the verb yāṣar is used predominantly with God as the subject,[5] in the Bible, bārāʾ, "created," is only used with God as the subject.

In Genesis 1, then, bārāʾ emphasizes God's unique relationship with what he has created. Specifically, it is used seven times in this first part of the creation story (1:1—2:4). Here in verse 1, it is part of a general introductory statement about creation. In verse 21, bārāʾ refers to God creating the tannînîm (sea monsters or great sea creatures), and so has the effect of transforming the ANE mythological belief of the great sea serpent,[6] which represented chaos, to be merely under God's creative power. The meaning is the mythical creature representing chaos is just a big fish (or "whale," KJV) God created in the sea. Three is the number of emphasis in biblical Hebrew and so it is significant for bārāʾ to be used three times when talking about the creation of Adam and Eve in verses 26-28. Bārāʾ also occurs with the first toledoth formula in 2:4.[7] Bārāʾ's use here connects the general creation story with the more intimate narrative about the creation of Adam and Eve. Importantly, seven is the biblical Hebrew number for completeness or perfection.

---

4. In Isa 45:18, God is said to have formed (yāṣar) the earth.

5. When yāṣar is used with people as the subject, it's often used to describe making idols (Isa 44:9, 10, 12; 45:9). In this passage, the expression of God "forming" (yāṣar) Israel occurs immediately before and after (Isa 44:2 and 44:21), what in technical terms is called an *inclusio*. In Isa 54:17 it refers to the one making weapons. In this example, God creates (bārāʾ) the smith who makes the weapons.

6. Tannin appears as a servant of Yamm (sea god), who is defeated by Baal (rain and fertility god) in the *Baal Cycle*, a Ugaritic myth (Pritchard, *Anthology*, 28-38). For a brief discussion, see Curtis, *Ugarit Ras Shamra*, 115. Some modern scholars link Tannin to Tiamat in the Babylonian creation myth *Enuma Elish*, which can be found in Pritchard, *Anthology*, 107-33.

7. The *Toledoth* formula is translated "this(these) is the account of/generations of" and divides Genesis into ten distinct sections (2:4—4:26; 5:1—6:8; 6:9—9:29; 10:1—11:9; 11:10-26; 11:27—25:11; 25:12-18; 25:19—35:29; 36:1—37:1; and 37:2—50:26).

Contours of Creation

The creation story, then, tells us of God (*Elohim*), who existed before the universe came into existence and alone is responsible for creating all things. This suggests that, as the creator, God has an intrinsic claim on and unique relationship with what he has created. This of course includes humans. Creation, however, is not a one-off act. Much of the modern debate about the creation account centers on the extent the naturalistic view of evolution contradicts the biblical account. Often overlooked is the question of what holds creation together. The question of why the totality of creation should continue in a sustained existence poses a problem for the naturalist. Why does creation not just dissipate or dissolve away? Why has creation not been met with an annihilation event—not just a small asteroid, but a planetary-sized smash, the damage from which would be irreversible?

For now, it will suffice to answer this question by noting that God does not leave what he has created to itself and merely wander off to a distant part of the universe, as a deist's conception of God would suggest. He sustains all things according to the purpose he has given each of them; "and it was so" follows each act of creation.[8] He has created all things through his Word and sustains them by his Word—the other miracle of creation (Heb 1:3). All things both living and non-living have a double dependence on God. He is their sole creator and sustainer. Humans occupy a unique place in creation. Genesis tells us about the initiatives God has taken in his relationship with people, how people have rejected God, and how God has set about to restore this relationship.

Who Is This Elohim?

The Hebrew term Moses uses for God in Genesis 1:1—2:3 is exclusively *Elohim*. *Elohim* was not only plural, which in itself could pose a problem for people who believed God was a single being,

---

8. The writer of Hebrews tells us (referring to the Son) that "he upholds the universe by the word of his power" (Heb 1:3). The same Word responsible for creating is responsible for upholding creation.

but the singular form, *El*, was the generic term for a god.[9] Moses lived in a world where pantheism and syncretism were the norm. Besides, growing up at Pharaoh's court under the shadow of the Egyptian gods, he eventually became the keeper of the stories passed down about Abraham, Isaac, Jacob, and Joseph, who had resided in Canaan. Non-biblical sources from around the same time as Moses indicate those at Pharaoh's court would have been familiar with *El* (a singular form of *Elohim*) as a common description associated with shrine gods of localities throughout Canaan.[10] The danger of a syncretic understanding of the *Elohim* of the Bible was a constant threat to the Israelites' knowledge and worship of God, even long after they had settled in Canaan.

However, Moses' experience of *Elohim* made it clear that the *Elohim* of creation was not just one of many competing gods. On Mount Horeb, also called the Mountain of *Elohim*, (Exod 3:1), Moses would learn that the transcendent God (*Elohim*) of the universe was the LORD (*Yahweh*), who reveals himself as deliverer of his people.[11] When Moses first turns aside to look at the burning bush, God identifies himself as the *Elohim* of Moses's fathers. Even though God has identified himself as the *Elohim* of Abraham, Isaac, and Jacob, Moses wants to know more specifically who *Elohim* is:

9. In the Bible the term *Elohim* can be used to refer to idols (Ps 95:3), angels (Ps 8), men (Gen 33:10), and rulers (Exod 21:6).

10. National identity and individual prosperity arising from associating with a particular god in a pantheon of competing gods was part of the way the ANE peoples viewed reality. An example from the Amarna letters (1360–1332 BC) shows the extent to which gods could cross borders. These letters were found in the ancient Egyptian capital Akhetaten and were written in Akkadian, the *lingua franca* of the time. Scholars have concluded that their writers spoke an early form of Canaanite. In letter 23, Tushratta, an Indo-European king, tells of his intention to send the Assyrian goddess Ishtar to heal Amenophis III of Egypt (Moran, *Amarna Letters*, 50). The polytheism and cult of El in Canaan is known through the archaeological findings at a place on the Mediterranean Sea, in modern-day Syria, which in ancient times was called Ugarit.

11. In the English-language Bible, *Yahweh* is translated in English as "LORD" to distinguish it from the Hebrew word *'ădonāy*, which refers to God, but is translated with an initial capital and then lowercase letters, "Lord." When this word refers to people, it is written as *ădonî* in the Hebrew and translated as lowercase "lord."

"... if they ask me what is his name? What shall I tell them?" God answers, "I am who I am."[12] In other words, he tells Moses to tell the Israelites that he is "the one who is." He is to be known as the foundation of existence and presence, incomparable and beyond human comprehension. This indefinableness of *Yahweh's* name not only gets the Israelites to look beyond the pantheism and syncretism that marked their existence, but meant that aspects of God's nature were also open to further disclosure. At this point in history, God says to Moses tell the Israelites that *Yahweh*, the *Elohim of their fathers*, has heard their cries of oppression and he will be with them to deliver them out of slavery.

When Moses eventually tells the intimate story of the creation of Adam and Eve in the garden of Eden (Gen 2:4–3), he will combine the name *Yahweh* with the name *Elohim* and exclusively use the compound name *Yahweh-Elohim* (LORD-God).[13] The *Elohim* who speaks the universe into existence is the *Yahweh* (LORD) who breathes life into the nostrils of Adam. The compound name connects the two different aspects of God. *Elohim* indicates the transcendent nature of God, whereas the name *Yahweh* captures his relational and covenantal nature, "This [*Yahweh*] is my name forever, and thus I am to be remembered throughout all generations" (Exod 3:15).[14] The transcendent *Elohim* who created all things is the intimate *Yahweh* who has entered into unique relationship with Adam and Eve. After their act of disobedience (the fall), the descendants of Adam and Eve divide into a spiritual seed descended from Seth and a carnal seed descended from Cain. *Yahweh* is the covenantal name that God uses to express his relationship with a particular people, the spiritual seed.[15]

12. Or "I will be who I will be."

13. Gen 2:4, 5, 7, 8, 9, 15, 16, 18, 19, 21, 22, 3:1. It is only in 3:2, with the temptation of Eve by the serpent, that the name *Elohim* is used by itself. Then in verse 8, after both Adam and Eve have eaten of the forbidden fruit, the name LORD-God is used. The LORD-God comes down to the garden to judge them.

14. The Septuagint translates *Yahweh* over six thousand times with the Greek word *Kurios*.

15. The terms *Elohim* and *Yahweh* occur almost equally in the book of Genesis, but not in the rest of the Bible. *Elohim* occurs 156 times in Genesis

Creation's Creator

Scholars starting in the nineteenth century used differences in the name of God in Genesis 1 and 2 to suggest two independent creation stories from different sources written at different times. Taken to an extreme, such literary proposals can make understanding who God is through his names a clever literary technique. A better explanation to me sees the differences in names reflecting the historical basis for God revealing himself as creator and as one who enters into relationship with people whom he has created. Bruce Waltke has noted the use of *Elohim* in Genesis 1 indicates that Genesis begins not as a tribal religion, but as a universal religion.[16] And as James Houston has noted, we must know God as LORD if we are to know him as *Elohim*, the transcendent creator,[17] which is exactly what Moses had learned.

Plurality within God: Is There a Case to Be Made?

Understanding the choice of the plural form *Elohim* as a name to describe the monotheistic God of Abraham has been a challenge to explain for some. Old Testament scholarship has explained the plural form in terms of its function as a plural of excellence, or a plural of majesty, as when a monarch might speak using the pronoun "we" in referring to herself or himself. Calvin preferred explaining the plural form in verse 1 as a plural of intensity that referred to God's powers. Grammatically, in the Hebrew, the use of singular verbs with the plural form *Elohim* shows that the writers of the Old Testament scriptures understood the plural form to refer to a single God. What is certain is that no one would argue that Moses who gave us the Ten Commandments was a polytheist.

---

and the name *Yahweh* 144 times. However, there is a disproportionate use when compared to the overall Bible. Around 23 percent of the use of the name *Elohim* occurs in Genesis, whereas only 2 percent of the use of *Yahweh* occurs in Genesis. Around 98 percent of the use of *Yahweh* occurs in the rest of the Bible. These statistics are from the Bible Works 10 software.

16. Waltke, *Genesis*, 24.
17. Houston, *I Believe*, 45.

But assuming that God wasn't a passive recipient of his name, we are still left with the question as to why he should choose the plural form instead of using only the singular form *El* or *Eloah*. We begin by noting that the Scriptures were not given to the nations but to the "faith" community. Our question may begin with the contingencies of the ANE world, but cannot end there. Therefore, we are also interested in exploring whether the plural form *Elohim* reflects the New Testament understanding of the nature of God as existing as three persons in one being. This question is closely tied to whether the initial picture of creation, with the Spirit of God hovering over the waters and *Elohim* speaking creation into existence, indicates the tri-personal nature of God.

We have seen how Moses's encounter with God at the burning bush led him to understand God not just as *Elohim*, the transcendent God of the universe, but as *Yahweh*, the covenantal God of relationships. Moses' new understanding only came about through his encounter and hence experience of God. The apostles continued in this tradition of "historical" revelation in their encounter of God. Their personal experience of God's salvation[18] revealed through the life, death, and resurrection of Jesus and the Holy Spirit's appropriation of this new reality in their lives led them to understand God as existing as one being in a tri-personal essence.

This new experience of salvation as encounter with the tri-personal God also allowed the apostles to understand God's acts of creation in the context of the tri-personal nature of God. These were Jewish believers who were thorough monotheists and would have been quite familiar with the creation story and its use in other parts of the Old Testament scriptures, in particular the worship book of Psalms. How they came to understand God's acts at creation did not change their understanding of God as one being, but rather clarified it.

---

18. In a general way salvation in the OT is seen as deliverance of the whole person from a temporal perspective. In the NT salvation is also seen as deliverance of the whole person, but in an unrealized eschatology. The focus in the NT is primarily on redemption from one's sins, but also points to the resurrection of the body when Christ returns.

CREATION'S CREATOR

The apostle Paul comes to recognize Jesus, the Son of God, not only as one who would offer himself as a sacrifice on the cross, but in his preincarnate existence, as the one through whom all things seen and unseen were created and hold together,

> For by him all things were created, in heaven and on earth, visible and invisible, *whether thrones or dominions or rulers or authorities*—all things were created through him and for him. And he is before all things, and in him all things hold together. (Col 1:16 17, emphasis added)

The apostle John, one of the inner three disciples who lived with and accompanied Jesus during his three years of ministry, begins his gospel:

> In the beginning was the Word [Jesus], and the Word was with God, and the Word was God. He was in the beginning with God. All things were made through him, and without him was not anything made that was made. (John 1:1–3)

To the apostles, Jesus was the agency of creation and was very God himself.

The apostles were also clear in their understanding of the Holy Spirit being more than merely the energy of God as he is mainly portrayed in the Old Testament.[19] They experience him as a distinct person.[20] It is the apostle Paul's experience of God and not abstract philosophy that leads him to see the connection between the tri-personal God who redeems people and the tri-personal God who has created all things. His post-conversion understanding of

---

19. The main reason for this may be that the Holy Spirit is the executor of the will of God and is portrayed as such in both Testaments.

20. W. H. Griffith Thomas points out that many religions understand God as a spirit, but Christianity is the only one that recognizes a "Spirit" in God. The NT writers associate the Spirit of God in the OT with the Holy Spirit. They experienced the Holy Spirit as not just the energy of God, but a distinct person. The Holy Spirit alone knows the mind of God (1 Cor 2:11). With the Father and the Son, he is the name in which people enter into the family of God (Matt 28:19) and are blessed (1 Cor 13:14). Some helpful works to explore this further are Fee, *Paul, the Spirit, and the People of God*, and Thomas, *Holy Spirit*.

redemption as appropriated by the person of Holy Spirit will be the true basis for understanding the regeneration of all creation. Adam through his disobedience had subjected creation to the curse: "Cursed be the ground because of you; in pain you shall eat of it all the days of your life" (Gen 3:17). Jesus, the second Adam, would redeem people and eventually liberate the creation itself (Rom 5:15–17). The apostle Paul shows how the Holy Spirit's ministry in the redemption of people and the liberation of creation are inseparably interwoven:

> We know that the whole creation has been groaning as in the pains of childbirth right up to the present time. Not only so, but we ourselves, who have the first fruits of the *Spirit*, groan inwardly as we wait eagerly for our adoption to sonship, the redemption of our bodies. (Rom 8:22–23)

The Holy Spirit who hovered over creation at the beginning now provides the link whereby the renewal of creation is seen in the context of his ministry of preparing the redeemed for the resurrection.

At the Beginning—a Good Place to See the Nature of God

We have seen how the New Testament writers came to understand the nature of God through their experience of him. This allowed them to understand the texts that speak of God as creator in a clarified way. In this section, we will explore how the plural form of the name *Elohim* and the picture we see of God at creation are related.

First, identifying the name *Elohim* here in verse 1 as indicating the tri-personal nature of God can be confusing. The picture given in the first three verses of Genesis has the Holy Spirit hovering over the chaotic waters and *Elohim* speaking creation into existence. The words are the creative agency of the Word (Son of God) himself. However, if we allow for the name *Elohim* to refer to the tri-personal nature of God here and insist the picture at creation shows each person of the Godhood distinctly, then reconciling these two understandings of God might cause some difficulties in a straightforward reading of the text.[21]

John Calvin would say that if we read the tri-personal nature of God into the name Elohim here, we would be falling into the danger of the error of Sabellius (*flor.* circa 220), who taught that the tri-personal nature of God was not really three persons, but three modes of God's operating.[22] To clarify Calvin's position, he believed the tri-personal nature of God could be referred to in the name *Elohim*, just that it wasn't being described in the use of the name *Elohim* in Genesis 1:1–3. Rather the plural form was a means to show an intensification of God's powers. However, Calvin does see the tri-personal nature of God reflected in the plural form *Elohim* in verse 26, "And Elohim said, 'Let us make man in our own image,'" since this statement implies the plurality of persons.[23]

In other words, the plural form *Elohim* can indicate the tri-personal essence of God, but this is not explicitly communicated through the grammatical plurality of *Elohim* alone. Rather, how God is being portrayed must be determined on a case-by-case basis that must be interpreted by context. In the case of Genesis 1:1–3, where *Elohim* speaks creation into existence, *Elohim* can best be identified as God the Father. This seems to be the general use of the term God in the New Testament, as when the apostle Paul will say in the grace benediction, "May the grace of the Lord Jesus Christ, and the love of God, and the fellowship of the Holy Spirit be with you all" (2 Cor 13:8). It's clear that for Paul the name *God* stands for God the Father here. The earliest Christians understood the nuances of the tri-personal nature of God. In the Apostle's Creed they formulated their understanding of the creator as, "I believe in God the Father, almighty, maker of heaven and earth."

---

21. Augustine's interpretation of verse 3 warns us of trying to penetrate this mystery too literally. He interprets the words "Let there be light" as spoken to God the Son and not God the Son himself (*On Genesis*, 157).

22. Calvin, *Genesis*, 59. Sabellius's teachings were quickly rejected as heretical by the early church because they were inconsistent with the biblical witness.

23. Calvin, *Genesis*, 73–74.

The brilliance of the plural form *Elohim* is that it can uniquely capture the monotheistic God of the Bible while at the same time contain the capacity to portray the tri-personal essence of God. So, while the plural form does not necessitate a tri-personal understanding of God, it naturally allows for it. When we interpret passages in Genesis and other parts of the Old Testament that use the name *Elohim*, how God is revealing himself in that particular historical situation must be understood through the biblical revelation of both the Old and New Testaments. As previously mentioned, the New Testament Jewish writers were thorough monotheists. After their personal encounters of God, they came to understand the Old Testament passages that speak about God with a clarity that had been veiled before the advent of Christ and the outpouring of the Holy Spirit at Pentecost. Importantly, they came to understand God in a way that was consistent with Moses' progressive encounter with God, which led him to know the transcendent God *Elohim* was the intimate God *Yahweh*. Christians who follow Moses and the apostles are not merely superimposing New Testament ideas[24] onto the Old Testament understanding of God. Rather, because of their own personal experience of God, they are seeing clearly what the writers of the New Testament understood and recorded.

What Else Can We Know?

With this in mind, depicting God acting in his tri-personal nature at creation provides insight into the inner relating of the persons of the Godhead. To provide more context, we first turn to the New Testament, where the writers reveal a picture of Jesus doing the will of God the Father and the Holy Spirit executing that will.[25] In the context of his ministry to redeem people, Jesus says that the Holy Spirit is sent by both the Father and himself. Yet, the New Testament also portrays each of the three persons as having

---

24. What sometimes in academia is called "supersessionism."

25. John 6:28; 14:31; 14:26; 15:26; Rom 8:27; 1 Pet 1:2. It must be noted that love is the fundamental means of relating.

a distinct will.[26] There is a seamless harmony and commonality of purpose in the expression of the will of each person.

At creation, we see this same harmony and commonality of purpose. The Holy Spirit hovers over the chaotic waters in the midst of darkness, waiting patiently for the initiation of creation by the Father. The Father speaks creation into existence through the agency of the Son, who accomplishes the Father's will. The Holy Spirit, who is hovering over the waters, acts in unison to execute the will of both the Father and the Son. The events of creation pull back the veil and allow us to see each person within the Godhead acting in unison to bring about creation. Theologians call the working of this inner relationship the "economy of God."

Why would the picture of the tri-personal nature of God occur at creation? We would be on good ground to assume that Adam and Eve, before the fall, would have naturally experienced God as tri-personal. It was only after the fall that the understanding and articulation of this dimension of God would have become opaque. When Adam and Eve willfully disobeyed God, sin became embedded in human nature. One of the consequences of this sinful disposition is a distorted way people understand the origin and purpose of creation.

The problem of sin was temporarily dealt with in the Old Testament under the sacrificial system, which was a shadow or type of what was to come. The writer to Hebrews tells us, " . . . it is impossible for the blood of bulls and goats to take away sins" (Heb 10:4). Christ would deal with the problem of sin once and for all through his death on the cross (Heb 10:11–12). This act of redemption, originating in God's eternal plan, in the truest sense revealed the nature of God, which had been indiscernible because of humankind's sinful disposition. The act of redemption was efficacious in saving us from our sins, and performed publicly in a way that glorified God in his true tri-personal essence.

We shouldn't mistakenly think that the tri-personal nature of God is merely a novel New Testament midrashic type of teaching.

---

26. The distinct "will" of the Holy Spirit, for example, is seen in John 14:26 and Rom 8:27.

The Holy Spirit bore testimony to the truth of God's nature during the Old Testament period. The apostle Peter makes us aware that what the prophets were experiencing was the tri-personal God, for they prophesied through the "Spirit of Christ" (1 Pet 1:11). However, before Christ came, and before his self-revealing act of sacrifice on the cross, they could not clearly understand or articulate it. The disciples only fully came to understand who God is through their personal experience of redemption in Jesus Christ (Heb 1). The problem of sin had to be dealt with decisively.

God's true nature was once again made evident when the eternal Son took upon himself flesh, fulfilled the righteousness of God through his death on the cross, and upon his ascension to the right hand of God the Father sent the eternal Spirit. Creation, as we will see in verse 3, is an expression of God's glory. It should come as no surprise that the very first description of God in the Bible is given in pre-fallen creation and reveals God in his full tri-personal nature and glory.

In concluding, Christians bring the Old Testament and the New Testament witnesses to the nature of God to the texts in Genesis in order to more fully understand the deeper dimensions of who *Elohim* is. To read the text inside this framework gives fuller meaning to God's acts throughout history, as given in the biblical story. At the same time, God worked through a historical process and the biblical text speaks to that historical reality. God met and revealed himself to real people at their place of need and in accordance to his plan to redeem people from their sinfulness. To read the text with a deeper understanding into the nature of God is not to ignore the historical reality of God's self-revelation through his particular deeds; rather it gives that historical reality a deeper meaning.

There comes a point where our rational capacity is limited in penetrating the mystery of God's nature. We shouldn't be surprised, though, because life is full of rationally unexplainable events. We do not have the capacity to explain the origin of creation—how things seen and unseen came into existence from non-existence (a question framed in ancient Greek ontology). Still, to say that creation's origin or the nature of the creator can't be known through rational capacity is not the same as saying they can't be known. Rather, it means that they have to be known through a different means. Christians believe this source of knowledge comes from God taking the initiative to share himself and his mighty deeds with us in a way that we can comprehend. This is what is meant by biblical revelation. By faith one enters into the life-changing reality of this mystery of God's self-disclosure. The tri-personalness of God is not about abstract philosophy, but a reality that I experience through God's gracious salvation and is reflected in the mystery of how all things were created and are upheld.

3

Ontology and Darkness

The earth was without form and void, and darkness was over the face of the deep. And the Spirit of God was hovering over the face of the waters.

—Gen 1:2

Greek philosophy originates as a breaking away from the Semitic world views held by its ANE neighbors. Thales, considered the first Greek philosopher, spoke of the world in terms of Babylonian thought, with the source of all things being a primordial body of water.[1] Thale's younger contemporary, Anaximander, whose critique of Thales is given to us by Aristotle in his work *Physics*, provides the move to abstraction that goes beyond our senses. This is the beginning of the Greek metaphysical philosophy that we are familiar with and the philosophy that would spur on Aristotle and eventually the Enlightenment thinkers. The ideas of the Enlightenment, in turn, have greatly influenced the way modern Western people pose questions about their world. These

---

1. Allen, *Thales to Aristotle*, 1–2. Like the Babylonian conception of creation, the biblical world is a primordial body of water. It exists formless and void and is covered by waters referred to as the "deep" ($t^e h\hat{o}m$).

ONTOLOGY AND DARKNESS

ways of thinking are often at odds with the Semitic concepts found in Genesis.

John Walton tells us that in Israel's understanding of the world, what he refers to as "cognitive environment," ontology was not material, but functional.[2] That is, the ANE creation myths did not seek to show a world coming into existence from a state of non-existence on a material basis, but rather on a functional and organizational one. So, a creation story like the *Enuma Elish* describes Marduk's activity as reorganizing the cosmos as much as creating the cosmos.[3] In contrast, Professor Walton notes that post-Enlightenment ontology has a material basis. People from the time of the Enlightenment on tend to express creation in the fiat ideas of its unseen and ultimate origin. They might ask "How did it get here?" and "What's its nature?" rather than "What function does it perform?" The reason ANE peoples were not interested in material ontology was not because they lacked curiosity. Rather, they believed that physical characteristics did not define an object's importance, but served as tools for the gods to carry out their purposes.[4]

A functional ontology may have been the focus of the ANE creation stories, but ANE people also understood an innate creative power contained in the spoken word.[5] For the Israelites this was the center or foundation to their understanding of reality. In the biblical account, the creative power of the Word of God is an expression of God's will that displays his goodness and love towards people.[6] The third-person commands that God issues, "Let there be . . . ," frame creation in reference to God. The intermediary between God and the coming into existence of creation is

---

2. Walton, *Ancient Cosmology*, 23. "Cognitive environment" is a shared way of thinking about the world.

3. Walton, *Ancient Cosmology*, 41.

4. Walton, *Ancient Cosmology*, 90.

5. As we will see with the example of Marduk in the *Enuma Elish*. See chapter 5, "And God Said."

6. See chapter 5, "And God Said." Creative power is not indiscriminate for God, but reflects his character.

the Word of his command. The author of the New Testament book of Hebrews speaks of the creative efficacy of the Word: "By faith we understand that the universe was created by the Word of God, so that what is seen was not made out of things that are visible" (Heb 11:3).

But this does not mean the Israelites held to a post-Enlightenment type of material fiat creation either. God, as the only source of existence, "I am who I am" (Exod 3:14), shows creation originating not from nothing, because the state of nothing does not exist in the minds of the biblical writers (Heb 11:3). All things are derived from God through his creative Word. It's the uniqueness of the creative Word emanating directly from God which links creation directly to God's existence. It is also the Word that sustains all of creation: "The Son is the radiance of God's glory and the exact representation of his being, sustaining all things by his powerful word."[7] Biblical ontology is the postulating of creation in relation to the existence of God. God is the source of existence, not just the organizer of chaos.

God chose to begin creation from a "formless and void" (*tōhû wābōhû*) earth, covered by waters referred to as the deep (*tᵉhôm*),[8] and in pitch blackness. We want to understand more specifically what this primordial earth represents. Outside of Genesis 1:2, the phrase *tōhû wābōhû* only occurs in Isaiah 34:11 and Jeremiah 4:23, in the context of judgment oracles. In Isaiah, the picture is one where the country of Edom will be completely desolated and become a desert, emphasizing its unfitness for living. When Jeremiah speaks against Judah, he also adds the distinction of there being no light in the heavens, no birds, and no people. Both uses of the phrase *tōhû wābōhû* emphasize places where people once thrived that would become uninhabitable for human life.

---

7. Heb 1:3. In the Genesis account the sustaining of all things is given by the phrase "and it was so." We discuss this in chapter 7.

8. The "deep" (*tᵉhôm*) refers to the primordial waters. They are the deep waters that burst forth during the flood in Gen 7:11. They are also the "deep" calling out to "deep" of Ps 42:7. In both Akkadian and Egyptian literature these waters are personified. See Walton, *Ancient Cosmology*, 144.

Ontology and Darkness

It is not the absence of all life that is being emphasized, but the absence of human life. In Isaiah, all sorts of desert creatures would populate Edom. Unclean birds such as desert owls, screech owls, and ravens, as well as jackals, hyenas and wild goats, and other night creatures, would thrive there. Jeremiah mentions there would be no people and all the birds of the sky would fly away, most likely referring to the exile of the inhabitants of Judah by their Babylonian conquerors. Jeremiah does not mention desert creatures, but he does refer to the land becoming a desert (Jer 4:26). Lastly, in Genesis 1:2 the *tᵉhôm* or deep waters that cover the earth are the same deep waters that burst forth during the flood in Genesis 7:11. God's judgment here involves returning the world (i.e., land) to a place that is uninhabitable.

The *tōhû wābōhû* in Genesis is a reference point from which to see the goodness of God. The transformation of the shapeless and formless world is done in such a way that emphasizes this was done with humankind in mind. People were never just one of many objects or creatures that God created. Rather, the creation story is told in such a way to show that humanity is the crown of creation. We see this in the buildup to the creation of Adam and Eve on the sixth day, and with the three uses of the term *bārāʾ*. The LORD-God places Adam in the garden he had already planted, one with all types of trees that were pleasing to the eye and good for food. God created the world and entrusted it to humankind out of his goodness.

The desolation of both Edom and Judah in the Isaiah 34 and Jeremiah 4 passages is not because of an unknown environmental catastrophe. The judgment on Edom was based on its hostility towards Israel.[9] In the case of the judgment on ancient Israel, they had no understanding and were skilled in evil (Jer 4:22). The flourishing of God's creation is closely tied to the moral uprightness of its inhabitants. Creation was meant to support those who reflected the glory of God. Since the fall (Gen 3) creation has been subjected to the sinfulness of humankind. The apostle Paul tells

---

9. For a sense of the animosity that existed between Edom and Israel, see 2 Sam 8:13–14; Lam 4:21; and Ps 137:7.

us that the whole of creation has been groaning in labor pains awaiting the revealing of the children of God (Rom 8:19–23). As humans become less than who they were created to be, they lose their ability to perform the mandate to steward creation. Isaiah and Jeremiah understood that the glory of creation is unfitting for those who don't reflect God's glory. These two prophets portray judgment as a world where the goodness of God has been removed, a world of *tōhû wābōhû*.

Finally, when talking about God's Word as the direct source of creation, there's an important distinction we learn about God from this picture of the primordial earth in verse 2. In the initial state of creation, God's Spirit is hovering over the deep amid the darkness and moving back and forth.[10] God is distinct from creation. He does not animate creation. Yet, the darkness that defines creation at this point does not exclude his Spirit. The darkness is not an absence of God and devoid of purpose.[11] Neither is there a complementary dualism of darkness and the light, which God will speak forth in verse 3, as is the case in the ancient philosophy of yin-yang or the ancient religion of Zoroastrianism. Darkness is subsumed to God's purposes. The biblical account of creation affirms that all of creation serves God's purposes, including darkness.

---

10. The verb in cognate Semitic languages is used of a hen brooding over her chicks.

11. The psalmist tells us that darkness is as light to God: "If I say, Surely the darkness shall cover me, and the light about me be night, even the darkness is not dark to you; the night is bright as the day, for darkness is as light with you" (Ps 139:11, 12).

4

A Poetry-Prose Hybrid

... the creation of the world was distributed over six days, for our sake, to the end that our minds might the more easily be retained in the meditation of God's works: ...[1]

—JOHN CALVIN

Day 1—*And God said*, "Let there be light..." (v. 3)
        And God saw that the light was *good*. (v. 4)
Day 2—*And God said*, "Let there be the sky..." (v. 6)
    <u>and it was so</u> (v. 7)
Day 3—*And God said*, "Let the waters be gathered. Let the dry land appear..." (v. 9)
    <u>and it was so</u> (v. 9)
    And God saw that it was *good*. (v. 10)
Day 3—*And God said*, "Let the earth produce all sorts of vegetation (v. 11)
    <u>and it was so</u> (v. 11)
    And God saw that it was *good*. (v. 12)

---

1. Calvin, *Genesis*, 73.

Day 4—*And God said*, "Let there be the luminaries in the sky (v. 14)
    and it was so (v. 15)
    And God saw that it was *good*. (v. 18)
Day 5—*And God said*, "Let the waters team with fish and the skies with birds (v. 20)
    And God saw that it was *good*. (v. 21)
Day 6—*And God said*, "Let the earth send out domestic and wild animals (v. 24)
    and it was so (v. 24)
    And God saw that it was *good*. (v. 25)
And God said, "Let us make man in our own image.(v. 26)
    And God *blessed them*. (v. 28)
And God said, "I give to you all plants . . . (v. 29)
    and it was so (v. 30)
    and behold, it was *very good*. (v. 31)

How we choose to interpret the creation account is related to the expectations we bring to the text. In the introduction, we discussed the larger sociocultural influences that have shaped the way we read Genesis. We also tried to critique the ungrounded idea that the literary genre of the creation story is only concerned with presenting the right ideas about God, but unable to tell us any "facts" about the origin of the world we live in or how God created it. Both cultural influences and expectations on how to read a particular genre create difficulties in reading the text.

On a practical level, in our modern specialized societies we compartmentalize disciplines. Science is science and poetry is poetry. In scientific writing we expect precision, logic, and order. These traits are values found in "rational" Western cultures. On the other hand, in poetic writings we admire a creative and unbound imagination. Creativity and its expression are also important values in Western cultures. Nevertheless, we expect explanations about creation to be written in scientific form. Since the Enlightenment we have been conditioned to believe that the discipline of modern science alone can describe objective truths about our world.

A POETRY-PROSE HYBRID

To be sure, the creation account has a type of modern scientific nuance to its classification of the world. The ancient Hebrews saw the universe as existing in three distinct spheres. There was the "firmament of the heavens" (all space above the earth), the land, and the sea. *Elohim* calls forth each sphere into existence and fills it with its respective creatures. Creation also progresses over seven days and so shows the chronological progression we would expect in a historical-based story. However, God's creative acts are given to us in a literary style that is a hybrid of poetry and prose. The biblical creation account includes repetition and a defined structure and other characteristics we expect to find in Hebrew poetry.

Perhaps this is why to us moderns the account of creation seems so puzzling. Not only does it not answer all the scientific type of questions that we bring to the text, but the events it reports are not done in the type of scientific way we would suggest it should be.[2] We've been conditioned to think that scientific language alone is the proper way to describe creation. But can scientific language alone capture the inexpressible aspects of nature? Can a methodology that operates only in a closed world adequately describe a holistic spiritual and physical world together? Does using both poetry and prose portray the nuance of God's ineffable glory in creation more than by using only one of the two forms of literature? How we answer these questions will influence the sensitivity we bring to the text.

The pragmatic truthfulness of the biblical creation account derives from the events of creation having dependency and meaning in relation to the tri-personal God. As moderns, our difficulty in understanding the creation story seems to be how we read the text. We have been conditioned to first ask, "How does the body of scientific knowledge that I hold to be true inform me as I read the biblical creation story?" Usually, we get stooped by bringing certain questions to the text, like "What happened to the dinosaurs?" In contrast, a faith-based reading starts with the text as it comes to us in hybrid literary form, of poetry-prose and

---

2. The creation account moves from dark to light, formlessness to form and emptiness to fullness, all within the framework of seven days.

in the modified genre of ANE creation stories, yet also depicting actual events that occurred—God created the earth that I live in. The biblical creation account is about an actual event and not just a transformed memory. A faith-based reading, then, lets the text shape the contours of our questions and imagination. The literature is never the end of our focus, but a means to draw us into the actual events and their meaning as they reveal what God wants us to know about himself, creation, and ourselves.

We proceed recognizing that the repetition of the phrases "And God said," "and it was so," "and God saw . . . good" gives the creation account a highly organized and repetitive literary pattern. Our focus over the next three chapters will be on the meaning of these three phrases that shape our understanding of God and his creative acts.

5

Words that Matter

In the beginning was the Word and the Word was with God, and the Word was God. He was in the beginning with God. All things were made through him, and without him nothing was made that has been made.

—John 1:3

Since Tim Berners-Lee invented the World Wide Web in 1990, generations have grown up being able to press a button and circulate personal information to large groups of people in a matter of seconds. Although the benefits of a more convenient way of life are easily seen in things we do, like banking and shopping, the social impact of this impersonal way of interacting is not exactly known.

Social Networking Service (SNS) platforms make it easy to share the most important personal and meaningful events, but in a matter-of-fact way. At times, the nuance can seem as impersonal as a major company's marketing platform for a new product. As one of hundreds connected to the same SNS site, we get the cold hard facts about someone's newborn child, a friend's camping trip, or even a family member's promotion. The computer has become the impersonal intermediary and the platform has shaped a generic message. The *you* of communication has become an *it*.¹ It may be that this new form of communication is leading to a greater sense of alienation than connectedness.

It's no surprise, then, in an age when the ability to communicate with others is so immediate that some young people seem to be yelling for attention, but feel as if they are not being heard. An impersonal message on a computer can never give relational value to a person who longs to interact in a way in which she is heard, understood, and acknowledged in the context of her unique personhood. Rather than feeling more connected, personal information on a computer screen can lead to a greater sense of alienation for those who must watch it and long to be part of "it." Meaningful relationship with another unique person involves a reciprocal and appropriate level of intimacy. Generic information on a computer screen can never replace this very basic human need.

In the biblical account, we are given two distinct pictures of how God creates. In the first, *Elohim* transforms the initial chaotic conditions of creation through speaking his Word. This includes the creation of humans. In the second, the more detailed perspective of the creation of Adam and Eve (Gen 2:5ff.), the LORD-*Elohim yāṣar* (forms/fashions) Adam from the dust and breathes into his nostrils. Afterwards, Eve is formed from the "rib" of sleeping Adam.

These different pictures of God creating show God to contain in himself the capacity for personal relationship. God's capacity for relational understanding of people, not just impersonal knowledge, and the capacity for intimacy are communicated to us in each part of the creation story. We will focus here on the general significance of God creating the world through his Word, and in a later chapter discuss in more detail the significance of the more detailed account of God creating Adam and Eve.

The refrain "And God [*Elohim*] said" is used nine times in the creation story in chapter 1.² The first seven times, God speaks

1. As in Martin Buber's *I and Thou*.
2. The fact that it doesn't occur at all in Gen 2 may also be evidence that

directly into existence all things other than human life. He calls forth his light to expel darkness, order to shape formlessness, and fills the emptiness of the land, sea, and sky with abundance. The word "swarming" (ESV) or "teeming" (NIV) and the commands to "be fruitful" "multiply" and "fill" describe the initial abundance of life on earth. In biblical Hebrew, seven is the number of perfection or completeness. Perfection in the sense of completeness of design and purpose, rather than according to exhaustive modern scientific concerns, seems to be the focus of God speaking the non-human creation into existence.

God's creative speech is command. "Let there be . . . " is a direct expression of the creative energy of the Son in response to God's will. There is no intermediary. God speaks into existence the three spheres of creation and fills them. However, this creative Word is set in the context of the personalness of understandable speech. In contrast, in the ancient world words were believed to have an impersonal power to change the material world. Words in the context of religion worked by moving deities, which were for the most part immoral and lived in an unseen reality. It was believed the gods could influence the natural elements and ensure a good crop or affect the outcome of war and bring a military victory. They merely needed to be cajoled and manipulated by the devotee.[3]

Words were also thought to have power in themselves in the form of pure magic. The gods themselves provide the example of this manipulative power innate in words. In the creation epic *Enuma Elish*, the god Marduk wants to prove his divine power and so he commands something to appear and then to vanish again.[4] Marduk is simply demonstrating the primary tenant of those who practice magic, that words have a dynamistic power in

---

we are dealing with one creation account and not two. The expression occurs nine times in Gen 1, far more than in any other chapter of the Bible. In Genesis, the expression "and God said" has around 50 percent of its total occurrences in the OT.

3. As is seen in Elijah's confrontation with the prophets of Baal in 1 Kgs 18:20–40.

4. Von Rad, *Theology*, 2:143.

and of themselves. Magic spells use words as a means to an end disconnected from any type of personalness. Because words have indiscriminate power in and of themselves, whoever repeats the words has the capacity to unleash their power.

Magic is the ultimate act of trying to usurp the creation from its creator. It is an impersonal speech that aims to manipulate nature or people independently of God, who sustains all things by his Word (Heb 1:3). "Rebellion is like the sin of divination" (KJV: "witchcraft), Samuel tells us (1 Sam 15:23). In contrast to speech that tries to manipulate or wields indiscriminate impersonal power, God's speech involves a relational purpose. His speech is an expression of the personalness of the Son to create the world that he entrusts humans to rule in his stead. The nature of how he creates—through the Word—communicates the capacity for intimacy and his desire for people to know this.

The eighth time God speaks, it is to share his intention to create humans. Command becomes the personal act of deliberation; "Let there be" becomes "Let us make." This phrase is best understood as God addressing himself in the diversity of his tri-personal unity.[5] That is, in his deliberation of creating humans, God's speech reflects the personalness of his nature. The ninth time, God speaks *with* the humans he has created and not *at* them. Communication is something that is shared alone with the humans and the capacity to communicate through speech with God is contained in what it means to be human. God speaking into existence through his Word implies that God can and does communicate personally. The very act of creation is an act of personalness, of God sharing himself through his Word.

Some philosophers of language would argue that we cannot know what God wished to communicate because he is a different being all together. They would suggest that there is no category of human thought or language that would have been adequate to

---

5. See chapter 1. The three choices are 1) a plural of majesty, 2) the heavenly council, which included angels, and 3) the triune God, whose true nature would have been clearly perceived by pre-fallen humankind. Gen 5:1–3 suggests that this is not a plural of majesty or a council of angels.

describe what occurred at creation. Neither Moses nor anyone else could have understood the incomprehensibleness of what occurred. This form of thinking leads to deism, which was proposed by men like John Locke, who belonged to the first generation of Enlightenment thinkers. God exists, but in some distant galaxy far from the workings of everyday creation and the lives of people.

In contrast, the beginning of the creation story reveals that the creator God speaks. God's communication is an expression of his own initiative, which is sometimes spoken of as his "providence." He does not sit passively somewhere in deep space waiting for humankind to engage him. Should he choose not to speak to us, we would have no means of knowing anything truthful about him, creation, or ourselves. God's speech expresses the engaging personal nature of God. Our speech is always in response to God's. This is inherent in the meaning of command, which originates with God. Our difficulty with hearing God's Word is a result of the nature we have inherited through the disobedience of Adam and Eve, a topic we explore later.

For Christians, God's communication at creation through his Word takes on a deeper meaning. They understand this Word to be none other than Jesus the Messiah. The Gospels make a clear the link between this creative Word at the beginning and the Word come in flesh. The apostle John uses a type of tautological reasoning at the beginning of his gospel. He tells us that Jesus is God's "Word" and that all things were created through him. Then in John 1:14 he says, "And the Word became flesh and dwelt among us, and we have seen his glory, glory as of the only Son from the Father, full of grace and truth." The Word spoken at the beginning of creation was not mere impersonal speech, but the personal agency of God the Son. In Jesus, God's personal Word of creation and the Word of redemption are joined together. The God who speaks creation into existence speaks this same Word through the life, death, and resurrection of his Son.

6

THE GLORY OF GOD

In their case the god of this world has blinded the minds of the unbelievers, to keep them from seeing the light of the gospel of the glory of Christ, who is the image of God. For what we proclaim is not ourselves, but Jesus Christ as Lord, with ourselves as your servants for Jesus' sake. For God, who said, "Let light shine out of darkness," has shone in our hearts to give the light of the knowledge of the glory of God in the face of Jesus Christ.

—2 COR 4:4–6

IN THE STUDY OF religions, one of the questions asked is to what extent God or gods inhabit creation. In some religions, there is no personal creator; rather there is an impersonal spirit or a sort of creative energy that pervades the universe. One example is the concept of the Atman-Brahman in Hinduism, where there is no creator or creature, only an absolute reality that is everything.[1] In contrast, a religion like Shintoism teaches that Kami (gods or spirits) can be found in anything animate or inanimate. The

---

1. Nigosian, *World Faiths*, 260. "There is the Atman-Brahman, an absolute reality and insists there is no creator and creature, just simple identity of everything. Expressed in the famous formula 'That are Thou.'"

The Glory of God

Kami can be people, birds, trees, rocks, mountains, and basically anything that has superior power, whether good or bad, or anything with an awe-inspiring ability.[2]

In the Genesis account, God precedes and stands apart from creation, but at the same time his eternal power and divine nature can be seen in creation (Rom 1:20). Another way of saying this would be that creation reflects God's glory. God's glory is his attributes that overflow[3] from himself and can be seen in his works, eliciting an awe-inspired, astounded response.[4] People were meant to look at creation and make inferences about the attributes of the creator. A limited analogy might be how the work of a gardener leaves traces of the gardener's character. We can tell from looking at a garden whether a gardener is given to detail, diligent, creative, etc. However, God's original creation only has a morally good quality because he is morally good. God pronounces this verdict on all that he has made: "It was very good."[5]

Although our interaction with creation was meant to leave us awe inspired, the reality of how people respond is somewhat different. After Adam and Eve disobeyed God, human nature became corrupted. People could no longer understand that creation was communicating knowledge of the glory of the creator. Their new constitution, one that was tainted with sin, caused them to confuse the glory of God with the creation itself. Their lack of understanding increased to the point where they started to worship the creation in the form of idols. This natural tendency to pervert creation is reflected in the first commandment, "Thou shalt not make unto thee any graven image, or any likeness of anything that is in heaven above, or that is in the earth beneath, or that is in

---

2. H. Byron Earhart quotes the "great" eighteenth-century Japanese scholar Motoori Norinaga (Earhart, *Religion in the Japanese Experience*, 10).

3. Christian theologians have regarded God's glory in different ways. Karl Barth has described it as indwelling joy overflowing. Hans Urs von Balthasar refers to it as an overflowing of self-giving love. (Fout, *Glory of God*, 1).

4. Exactly the healthy "fear" (*phobeomai*) and dumbfounded "marvel" (*thaumazo*) response of the disciples to Jesus commanding the storm to be still in Luke 8:22–25; Matt 8:23–27; Mark 4:35–41.

5. See chapter 8.

the water under the earth" (Exod 20:4, KJV), and captured by the apostle Paul in Romans 1.

As spectators, our view of creation begins when God commands light (*'ôr*) into existence.[6] However, for modern readers the creation of light on day one and then the creation of the sun and moon on the fourth day has caused more than a few raised eyebrows. Some biblical scholars would suggest that verse 3 and verses 14–18 are two different versions of the same event.[7] Understanding what happens on day one within a modern "scientific reading" is also a challenge. God calls forth light (*'ôr*) and separates it from the darkness. The light he calls "day" and the darkness he calls "night," and then we read there is evening and morning. We are left asking, how is it possible for there to be light before the sun is created on the fourth day and how is it possible for day one to be created within a day?

Before we propose how to understand the creation of light, it will be helpful to quickly review how creation progresses. The initial world exists in a state of chaos. In this state the world is in darkness. It is formless and void, covered by the deep waters. The first act of creation that we see is God dispelling the darkness. He then creates three distinct spheres (sky, land, and seas), which he subsequently fills with their respectful creatures or objects. However, God successively creates transforming the chaos into order and abundance over six days, and then on the seventh day he rests. *Elohim* transforms the world over seven days for our benefit and to reveal his nature to us. Any explanation of the creation of light must occur within this framework.[8]

---

6. The first use of light does not have the definite article, but the second use as a direct object does. Although there is not a definite fixed usage of the article in biblical Hebrew, there might be a parallel here with the use of the definite article in English. That is, the definite article is used in English after both people understand what is being referred to. The implication is that the first usage without the article has a "newness" to one of the parties.

7. In biblical scholarship this falls under the area of source criticism.

8. Some scholars downplay the chronological sequence of creation. They say that the lack of definite article on the word "day" in the Hebrew allows for a flexible translation.

The Glory of God

The Source of the First Light

What is the connection between the light created on day one and the light from the sun and moon on the fourth day? The word for "light" (*ʾôr*) that God speaks forth on day one is the same root word Moses uses to describe the sun, moon, and the light that comes from either on the fourth day. The sun and moon are called *mā-ʾôr* (luminaries). The sun is called the "greater *mā-ʾôr*" and the moon is called the "lesser *mā-ʾôr*." Biblical scholars have pointed out that a possible reason that the word for "light" is used instead of the names sun and moon is polemical. In ANE societies, the sun god (*Shamash*) and the moon god (*Yarich*) were two of the most important gods and their names sound very similar to the Hebrew word for the sun (*shemesh*) and moon (*yareakh*).[9] They say Moses wanted to avoid any possibility of implying polytheism. This may be true, but there seems to be another more fundamental and intentional explanation.

Rather than being an anomaly, the creation of light on day one and the sun on the fourth day shows that God is the ultimate source of light, as he is the source of all things, and to emphasize the fundamental nature of God—his glory. That is, the sun and other planetary bodies derive their light from its original source, *Elohim*. If we could hear the Hebrew, God's exclusive use of the word *ʾôr* creates this perspective. Not only does the word *ʾôr* connect the planetary bodies with the light on day one, but God imparts to the planetary bodies *mā-ʾôr*, the function of separating the day from the night (v. 14) and the light from the darkness (v. 18) that he himself carries out on day one (v. 4). They derive their functions because he appoints them by command. Command, again, connects all the aspects of creation. What God does on the fourth day is to impart the planetary bodies with the function of continuing the light of which he is the source.

The point is that before the creation of the sun and moon, God himself is *ipso facto* the direct source of the light. By calling forth light on day one, God dispels the darkness, which was part of the

---

9. Provan, *Dangerous Religion*, loc. 657.

original state of a formless and void world covered by waters. We are given this aspect of God's light through the standard formula, "Let there be ... And God saw that the light was good ... and he caused the light to be divided from the darkness ... and he called the light day ... " However, it's the connection with the term ʾôr in verses 14–18 and the chronological sequence of creation that draws one to realize that this light derives from no ordinary planet.

One of the main symbols the biblical writers use to express God's glory in the Bible is light (ʾôr). The psalmist says, "Thou *art* more glorious [*nā-ʾôr*] and excellent than the mountains of prey (Ps 76:4, KJV). Glorious here is ʾôr, "light," as a descriptive verb. Some of the newer English translations try to capture the aspect of light with "resplendent" (NAS) or "radiant with light" (NIV). The light is merely a way of speaking about the character or nature of God. In this sense, the word "glorious" is more consistent with the non-literal way ʾôr is interpreted in other passages of Scripture.

Consider the following from Isaiah 60:19-20:[10] "The sun [*shemesh*] shall be no more your light by day, nor for brightness shall the moon [*yareakh*] give you light; but the LORD will be your everlasting light [*lᵉ-ʾôr*] and your God will be your glory [*tip̄ ʾereṯ*]."[11] The parallelism between "light" and "glory" is a technique in Hebrew poetry that equates the two terms. The use of different words in the Hebrew to express God's glory lets us realize that no one word is capable of describing his ineffable glory. Perhaps most telling is John's use of the term "light" to describe God's glory in Revelation 21:23: "And the city has no need of sun or moon to shine on it, for the glory of God gives it light, and its lamp is the Lamb."

Other clues in the text help us to understand the first light in this way. We notice that on day one, after God commands light (ʾôr) into existence, there is no pronouncement "and it was

---

10. God's glory is portrayed as a light in Scripture: Isa 60:19; Luke 2:32; 2 Cor 4:6; Rev 21:23. Isa 60 has seven uses of the term ʾôr (Isa 60:1 [2x], 3, 19 [3x], 20).

11. The root for "glory" here is "beauty," which adds a dimension to what God's glory is.

so." There are only six "and it was so" expressions in the creation account, which give a finality and sustained purpose to each of God's creative speech-acts. God speaks the formula to show the completion of each of the spheres of creation (sky, land, and sea by implication), and the filling of those spheres (vegetation, non-human life), and the means of sustaining life (giving of vegetation for sustenance). All the three spheres of creation (sky, land, and sea) and all the teaming life within (plant and non-human life) have this sense of completion to them.[12]

The formula is missing from the speaking forth of light on day one. If we assume that the omission is purposeful, then might this light that God does not pronounce a finality to imply more than the greater and lesser lights created on the fourth day and from which they derive their light?

There is another curious element to this light. This light is the only element that God speaks into being from outside of the three spheres of existence (land, sky, and sea). In a certain way, it is a unique aspect of creation. Everything else originates within the three spheres of existence or in reference to them. On the second day, the sky involves the act of separating the waters vertically. On the third day, formation of the land involves separating the waters horizontally. The rest of creation (vegetation, planetary bodies, fish, birds, animals, and finally humans[13]) fill in and are closely associated with their respective spheres. The initial act of creation—as we are to understand it— does not focus on the creation of the sun's light, but rather God reveals himself to be the source of light.

There is another difference in the formula of creation worth noting—the use in Hebrew of the cardinal number one for day one alone.[14] All other days use ordinal numbers (second, third, fourth, etc.). The effect is to create a difference between day one and all

---

12. See Table 1 in chapter 7.

13. Humans stand unique—"Let us make humankind in our image"—but even they are created of the "dust" from the ground.

14. It is not uncommon for the number one to be used as a cardinal number in Semitic languages. But this might only support the fact that number one as the beginning of something was significant for ANE people.

the other days. The cardinal number could reflect that God is the primary source of all things and that all other days represented by ordinal numbers relate to this primary day. This may also explain why the formula for biblical days of creation begins with sunset—"and there was evening and morning"—and not sunrise as we would expect. As James Houston notes, perhaps the theological significance of this practice of starting the day with sunset and not sunrise is the theological affirmation that "the day, every day, begins with God the creator and not the natural agency of the sun."[15]

The order of placing God communicating his glory on day one is significant because God's glory stands prior to creation. It is not just God's presence hovering over the darkness that is a precursor to creation. But it is the communicating of God's glory as light to creation that stands as the real catalyst. In the act of creating, God first communicates his glory, which provides the light by which we can see all of creation, including the sun and moon and light that they give. Like the rest of creation, we were meant to see the light as a reflection of the one who created it. The biblical writers were able to see this clearly and so light is the means by which God's glory is captured. Karl Barth says the following about light as a prominent symbol of God's glory throughout Scripture: "Divine glory is the shining forth as light and the worth which is communicated in that shining forth: it is in fact God."[16]

Seeing More Clearly the Light of God's Glory

Full knowledge of God's glory cannot be derived from a fallen creation alone. Although Adam and Eve were able to see the glory of God in creation, heightened by their placement in the garden of Eden, we do not have the same privilege. In other words, creation's ability to reflect the glory of God has in some mysterious way been altered and shielded because of the sinfulness of humankind.

15. Houston, *I Believe*, 59.

16. Fout, *Glory of God*, 54. He is referencing Karl Barth's *Church Dogmatics*, II.1, 643.

The Glory of God

When people look at creation, they can no longer see the immediacy of God's glory.

To see the glory of God in creation requires a faith commitment in the LORD of creation.[17] The glory of the one who created all things is also revealed in the redemption of his people. The people of God waited for ages for the fulfillment of Isaiah's words, "... but in the future he will honor Galilee of the Gentiles ... the people walking in darkness have seen a great light" (Isa 9:1b–2). Christians understand Jesus, who was raised in Nazareth of Galilee and began his ministry in Galilee, to be the fulfillment of this prophecy and to be this great light (*'ôr gādôl*).

In 2 Corinthians 4:4–7, the apostle Paul will link the light spoken of at the beginning of creation (Gen 1:3) with Christ. He says that the light God speaks into the darkness of creation God makes to shine into our hearts. This light is the knowledge of the glory of God in the face of Christ. The writer to Hebrews says of the Son, "He is the radiance of God's glory and the exact representation of his being ... " (Heb 1:3, NIV). The true light of God's glory, which was seen in the original creation, is recovered and seen in the Lord Jesus Christ.

---

17. Houston, *I Believe*, 45.

7

THE CERTAINTY OF GOD'S WORD

Then the LORD answered Job out of the whirlwind and said:
"Who is this that darkens counsel by words without knowledge?
Dress for action like a man;
I will question you, and you make it known to me.
"Where were you when I laid the foundation of the earth?
Tell me, if you have understanding.
Who determined its measurements—surely you know!
Or who stretched the line upon it?
On what were its bases sunk,
or who laid its cornerstone,
when the morning stars sang together
and all the sons of God shouted for joy?
"Or who shut in the sea with doors
when it burst out from the womb,
when I made clouds its garment
and thick darkness its swaddling band,
and prescribed limits for it
and set bars and doors,
and said, 'Thus far shall you come, and no farther,
and here shall your proud waves be stayed'?

—JOB 38:1–11

The Uncertainty of Naturalism

DARWIN'S *THE DESCENT OF MAN* gives fascinating details about fish, amphibians, and birds. Darwin notes the distinguishing characteristics of the male and female within a species and tries to explain their relative redundancy in terms of being necessary for mating and the raising of young. Female fish tend to be larger than their male counterparts. Female birds tend to be smaller. Male birds have more colorful plumage and generally are better singers (according to Darwin) than their female counterparts in order to attract females. The result is a cause-and-effect explanation for those things that seem to serve no purpose in the bird's primary day-to-day survival, but serve to further the survival of the species. Hence, they are called "secondary sexual characteristics." But Darwin also points out that there are always exceptions. One of the many examples he gives is species of birds in which the size and plumage of the males and females do not significantly vary. This is precisely the point at which Darwin's arguments leave one feeling unconvinced. There are always exceptions to the rule.

In fact, Darwin accused others of having "arrogant" assumptions, but didn't realize that his conclusions, which are presented as objective and based on observable characteristics, are really supported by unprovable assumptions. Consider the following quote:

> It is only our natural prejudice, and that arrogance which made our forefathers declare that they were descended from demi-gods, which leads us to demur to this conclusion. But the time will before long come, when it will be thought wonderful that naturalists, who were well acquainted with the comparative structure and development of man, and other mammals, should have believed that each was the work of a separate act of creation.[1]

Darwin assumes that similarity between the physical characteristics of two species can best be explained by postulating a common ancestor or progenitor. However, this certainty of one

---

1. Darwin, *Descent of Man*, 25.

type of species transitioning into a different species can only be offered at a degree of probability and under certain assumptions. One example is Darwin's explanation of the human *os coccyx*, which is the tiny piece of spinal cord at the end of the spine that appears to serve no apparent use. He suggests that over the course of development the primate progenitors of humans wore off their tails by friction, i.e., sitting down.[2] Modern scientists have more leeway and can explain things from a disruption or corruption of DNA sequencing, which then produces the trait. The problem arises for naturalists because they must always assume there is a cause-effect relationship to explain why things are the way they are. They must also assume there isn't a personal creator, or if there is a creator, he is restricted by the cause-and-effect laws that he has created.

These assumptions are key for evolution. However, if we assume God is the creator with freedom to choose, then the contours of creation can look somewhat different. We could as easily assume that the similarity between the *os coccyx* in humans and the tail in chimpanzees originates from the work of this common creator. We might also say that the difference is intentional and not accidental, nor the result of cause and effect. We could just as easily assume that any similarity or difference points to the artistic style of the same creator, who created each separately with a distinct purpose in mind.

This type of reasoning is analogous with identifying the work of a famous artist. When we are shown the paintings of a famous artist, we are often able to identify it as the creation of that artist. "That's a Monet," we say without having seen the picture before. We are able to draw such a conclusion because the artist has a distinct brush stroke and a way of using colors that is commonly reflected in all of his paintings. We might also assume that the presence of an *os coccyx* has to do with functionality in one species and

---

2. "But what are we to say about the rudimentary and variable vertebrae of the terminal portion of the tail, forming the os coccyx? A notion which has often been, and will no doubt again be ridiculed, namely, that friction has had something to do with the disappearance of the external portion of the tail, is not so ridiculous as it at first appears" (Darwin, *Descent of Man*, 76).

nothing to do with functionality in another by design. There must always be assumptions when your ability to know something is not absolute. Once you remove God from any active involvement in creation, the observable data will be interpreted according to the assumptions held, even if the assumptions are held unknowingly.

Even if we were to accept Darwinian assumptions, there is only one conclusion that can be reached—"I think it was so." The uncertainty of the conclusions based on the interpretation of the evidence, which changes so frequently in modern humankind's quest for secular truth, couldn't contrast more with *Elohim*'s pronouncement "it was so."

The Certainty of Elohim's "It Was So"

Table 1: The Occurrence of the Phrase "and It Was So" Spoken by God during Creation

Day	Sphere of creation	"And it was so" formula	Day	Filling of sphere	"And it was so" formula
1	light	None; "and there was light"	3	Vegetation (v. 11)	yes
2	expanse or sky (v. 7)	yes	4	greater and lesser lights (v. 15)	yes
3	land (v. 9)	yes	5	fish, birds,	no, but its occurrence after the creation of land animals is perhaps meant to include fish birds and animals together as living creatures

					land animals (v. 24)	yes, after all types of non-human life is created
				6	humans	no; a possible indication that the account in Gen 2 is the same but more detailed account of humans being created
				6	sustenance for animals and humans	yes; God uses these words after he has provided sustenance for all life

The Genesis creation account tells us that God creates through his eternal Word. The way he creates, through speech, speaks of his ability and desire to communicate with us. He utters in third-person commands (called "jussives")—"Let there be"— which shows creation originates as an expression of his will or intention. However, it is not enough for God to speak creation into existence and hope for statistical probability to do its job, or to hope that what is created doesn't fall apart. This simple phrase "and it was so" shows that what God commanded came into existence as he intended and continues to exist according to the power of his Word. There is an exact correspondence between what God wills, the expression of that will, and what transpires. The end does not differ from the intended beginning. Nor does the beginning morph into a different end. What God willed was expressed through his Word and found perfect actualization as he intended it.

In Table 1, we see that *Elohim* speaks "it was so" six different times during creation. In the first two pronouncements of "it was so" *Elohim* establishes the boundaries of each of the three spheres of existence. On the second day, God establishes the expanse (sky and space) and then he pronounces "it was so."[3] On the third day he creates the dry land and then pronounces "it was so." Both acts of creation involve the dividing or gathering of waters. The idea here consists of creating the sky, land, and sea and maintaining their boundaries. God's pronouncement "it was so" marks out distinctly the completion of these three spheres of existence. God spoke to Job about these limits: "Where were you when I laid the foundation of the earth? ... Or who shut in the sea with doors ... " (Job 38:4, 8).

The contribution of this fixed non-living environment to support all species of life is significant. We see this clearly at the judgment of the flood, which we have already mentioned. At this time, God was grieved that he had made people because he saw "how great man's wickedness on the earth had become, and that every inclination of the thoughts of his heart was only evil all the time" (Gen 6:5, NIV). So God purposed to destroy all life through a flood. Only Noah found favor in God's eyes. The destructive forces of the judgment came from removing the boundaries that separated water from land. The flood gates of heaven and the flood gates of the deep were opened. God removed the boundaries that separated the waters above the експанse from below and that kept dry land and sea separate. Creation reverted to its primitive and disordered form of being a mass of deep waters ($t^e h\hat{o}m$).

Indeed, this picture is exactly what Moses wanted us to understand. The language and structure of the creation account has many parallels in language with the post-flood account of the resettlement of the earth. These similarities are not coincidental. They indicate that the stability of these larger spheres of existence determine species survival and that the existence of one species does not just depend on outmaneuvering another species for limited resources. The flourishing of life results from God creating and establishing an environment that supports life. Any questions about the origin and continuation of life must be seen in this larger context.

---

3. In the last chapter, we discussed the possible reason *Elohim* did not pronounce "it was so" after he dispersed the darkness on day one.

When we move to the filling of the sea, sky, and land with their respective creatures, we find three uses of *Elohim* pronouncing "it was so." On the third day, God commands the earth to bring forth vegetation according to its "kind" (*mîn*) and speaks "it was so." On the fourth day, God fills the expanse with the sun, moon, and distinct planetary bodies and then pronounces "it was so." Then after God creates fish, birds, and animals to populate each of the three respective spheres of existence, he pronounces "it was so." Through this last pronouncement, the animals that are created on the sixth day (as are humans) are categorized with the fish and birds, which are created on the fifth day. God's decree "it was so" marks out distinctly the creation of the inhabitants that fill each of the spheres.

To be sure, the creation account is not given as a modern scientific textbook. The phrase "according to its kind" (*mîn*) does categorize species, although not in the language that is used to describe living species in modern biology.[4] Then again, we wouldn't have expected Moses to use modern scientific language in his three-thousand-year-old account of creation. But we shouldn't dismiss the picture that is being presented. It is only the living creatures, the plants and animals, and not the planetary bodies that are created according to their (*mîn*) kind.[5] There is a clear distinction being made in the created order between the living and non-living. The living order has an innate ability to replicate according to each individual's kind. The non-living order lacks this characteristic. In naturalism, at some point in time there must be a transition from non-living to living. This type of world doesn't exist in the Genesis story.

There is also another distinction given to the created living animals. In addition to the phrase "according to its kind," which describes the diversity of animal life, Adam will name each of

---

4. See under *mîn* in Harris et al., *Theological Wordbook of the Old Testament*, 1191a. The authors imply that *mîn* does not refer to fixed species. I suggest that in an indirect way it does.

5. The phrase "according to its kind" (*lᵉ-mîn-ô*) might be better translated "every different kind" and emphasize all the diversity of life. Neville, *Differentiation in Genesis 1*, 209–26.

the animals. This naming has several functions, one of which is to acknowledge the distinctness of each kind of animal. This is done before God creates Eve and so before the fall. In other words, prior to sin entering the world through the disobedience of Adam and Eve, the land species seem to have been fixed. All life which abounded with diversity and fecundity had distinct boundaries "according to its/their kind." Overarching these boundaries, there is a definiteness that is portrayed by God's pronouncements of "and it was so."

In summary, God's use of the phrase "it was so" has at least two nuances to it. Its first five uses mentioned above point to a finished component of God's creation. He speaks forth and it comes to be in its completed form in unique purposefulness. This involves the non-living creation, which supports but is distinct from the living creation. The diversity that God has created "according to its kind" has a definiteness to it. However, in the sixth and last usage there is a slightly different nuance.

The sixth pronouncement occurs not after God creates Adam and Eve, but after he has allocated vegetation as food for all living things. In this instance there is the future idea of continuing or sustaining what he has created. Every aspect of creation attains a finality and unique purposefulness, but for life that relies on other life for survival, embedded is God's decree to continue existing. That is, the dynamic continuance of life is sustained by God's creative pronouncement. The certitude indicated in God's words goes beyond the explanation given by observable characteristics. It is forward effecting and guarantees the necessary sustenance for the continuance of life. This formula, with its present and future nuances that speak to the sustaining of life, stands in contrast to naturalistic explanations that observe and describe with probability.

The sustaining activity of the expression "and it was so" is balanced by the life-giving words "and God blessed." This latter phrase God speaks only on living species, first on the fifth day with the fish and birds, and then with humans. Noticeably, it is not used with land animals, even though it is used on the fish and birds. The reason may be that animals share the same sphere of existence as humans and are subjugated to human rule. Fish and birds are also subjugated to human rule, but they occupy their own spheres of existence. The flourishing of animals is done within the context of sharing the earth with the humans. However, animals are not the equal of humans.[6]

The term "blessing" is the communication of a life force to enable living species to continue and replicate. Blessing imparts the energy and capacity to flourish, and "it was so" adds to the sustenance of this capacity. There is nothing here that indicates life is left on its own to chart its own path. Rather, God's words reveal that he not only gives the ability for all life to multiply and expand, but he also is responsible for its continuance. The picture we get is of an active creator who wills his creation to exist and sustains it in abundance.

There is a certitude to God's Word that is unknown in our use of words. Sin has marred creation and even challenged the "it was so" of God's Word. The extinction of species is an inevitable outcome in a world that has been groaning under the bondage of sin. However, the same Word through whom all things were created now becomes the Word who took upon himself flesh and through whom all things will be reconciled to God. Jesus says about the enduring steadfastness of his words, "Heaven and earth will pass away, but my words will not pass away" (Matt 24:35). The "it was so" that describes the original creation finds its fulfillment in Jesus, who became the "it was so" final Word of God (Heb 1:1–3).

The apostle Paul tells us, "he made known to us the mystery of his will according to his good pleasure, which he purposed in Christ, to be put into effect when the times reach their fulfillment—to bring unity to all things in heaven and on earth under Christ" (Eph 1:9–10). When God raised Christ from the dead, he put all things under his feet and "appointed him to be head over everything for the church which is his body, the fullness of him

---

6. A proper carrying out of God's charge to humankind as stewards of creation guarantees the proper treatment of animals. Animals are the Lord's: "For every beast of the forest is mine, the cattle on a thousand hills." (Ps 50:10).

who fills everything in every way" (Eph 1:22–23, NIV). The final plans of the church and the final plans of creation are not separate. Christ will redeem his people and subsume all things and return them to God. The creation which has been subjugated to the sinfulness of humankind will be transformed. In the new heavens and new earth (Rev 21:1), the original "it was so" is realized as the final "it was so" through Christ Jesus.

8

MISSING THE GOOD GOD SEES IN CREATION

Here, O my people, listen as I speak.
  Here are my charges against you, O Israel:
  I am God, your God!
I have no complaint about your sacrifices
  or the burnt offerings you constantly offer.
But I do not need the bulls from your barns
  or the goats from your pens.
For all the animals of the forest are mine,
  and I own the cattle on a thousand hills.
I know every bird on the mountains,
  and all the animals of the field are mine.
If I were hungry, I would not tell you,
  for all the world is mine and everything in it.
Do I eat the meat of bulls?
  Do I drink the blood of goats?
Make thankfulness your sacrifice to God,
  and keep the vows you made to the Most High.
Then call on me when you are in trouble,
  and I will rescue you,
  and you will give me glory. —PS 50:7–15

Missing the Good God Sees in Creation

THE DEVASTATING EARTHQUAKE AT Lisbon in 1755 was the rallying point for Enlightenment philosophers like Voltaire to challenge the idea of a benevolent creator. The earthquake left Lisbon ravaged with collapsed buildings, fires, and the devastating aftereffect of a tsunami. To make matters worse, the earthquake happened on the religious holiday of The Feast of All Saints. Thirty to fifty thousand people are reported to have lost their lives. Forty-five years before this event, the German philosopher-mathematician Gottfried Leibniz had coined the term "theodicy" to refer to arguments that try to resolve the problem posed by the presence of evil in a world in which God is all-powerful and good. Theologians usually make a distinction between moral evil (evil committed by people) and catastrophic events that cause harm, which they refer to as "natural evil"[1] (of the type which occurred in Lisbon). Our focus in this chapter will be on what the biblical witness means when God sees the creation is "good."

A Human-Centered Definition of Good

If we were left to our own experiences of creation, we might be inclined to define the term "good" as something that brings us pleasure. We might say golden sunsets, the colorful plumage of birds and the bright patterns on fish, the smell of roses, the peaceful sounds of an isolated lake early in the morning, the feeling of a smooth stone between our fingers, or even a mouthful of our favorite food are, according to this definition, good. However, we would also be confronted with details about creation that wouldn't fit into our definition of "good," such as swamps, rotting carcasses, the smell of skunks, blobfish, the shrilling cries of a lynx, or the thistles on a rose bush. As one teenager so aptly said, all the things that make us go "ew!"

In contrast, we could define the term "good" to mean whatever doesn't harm me. But then we are confronted with volcanoes, tsunamis, sink holes, great white sharks, murder hornets,

---

1. Sometimes theologians use the term "surd evil."

mosquitoes, poisonous berries, and the list goes on. According to this definition, these things would not be good. If these things existed in a way in pre-fallen creation as they do now—and the word "assume" is important—then in what way is it possible to say these things are good? Theologians have long debated and come up with different answers to whether the pre-fallen world would have been harmful to humans and whether the harm we perceive from these things is the result of moral evil being introduced into the world.

According to our definition, the meaning of "good" is dependent on a pleasant feeling that we experience through our interaction with creation or a beneficial function that creation provides to us. We could say that the basis for these definitions of "good" is creation's utilitarian role in serving us. However, we would need to clarify our definition. Actually, we can only really talk about something being good under certain conditions. The sun can give me a pleasant feeling while I watch it set in the evening and be an abundant source of vitamin D during the day, but too much sun can lead to sunburn and dehydration and, on a larger scale, draught and famine. In a similar way, a bird with beautiful plumage can become a rotting carcass, a magnificent-looking mountain can become the source of a devastating avalanche, and a tasty-looking berry can be lethal. What is common to these ideas of what is good in creation is they are defined from a human-centered perspective. We shouldn't downplay the importance of perspective. Bats thrive near large populations of the mosquitoes they eat, but humans can contract rabies and malaria from each respectively and want neither. The meaning of God asserting that all creation is good goes beyond the anomalies created by human-centric perspectives.

A Biblical Definition of Goodness in Creation

The biblical testimony defines goodness from a perspective that is outside of the closed world of the modern scientist and philosopher. God himself is the one who identifies the creation as good for us. In other words, creation derives its goodness from God.

Missing the Good God Sees in Creation

God's evaluation of the world as "good" (*tōv*) occurs seven times in the creation account in Genesis 1. As mentioned previously, the number seven is meant to represent perfection or completeness. God does not say the creation is "good." Rather, we are told in reported speech that "God saw [*wayyarʾ Elohim*] . . . was good."

The act of seeing is worth noting. Outside of the creation account, the very next time "*Elohim* sees" something is in Genesis 6:12: "God saw [*wayyarʾ Elohim*] how corrupt the earth had become, for all flesh had corrupted their way upon the earth." The comparison between the two uses of the expressions suggests the words "God saw" do not indicate discovery, as if he only became aware that creation was good after he had finished it. Rather, the words reflects his moral assertion—"good" in the case of the pre-fallen creation and "corrupt" in the case of a world contaminated with sin. The verb "saw" also portrays God directly engaged in creation without any intermediary.

There are several more observations we can make about the word "good" in the creation account. In the first use (v. 3) of the word "good" and the last use (v. 31), there is a specific Hebrew particle used to mark the direct object of the verb "see." The other five occurrences of the expression "and God saw" do not use this particle to mark the direct object. The reason could be that we are meant to understand the first and last use of "good" as bookends to create emphasis. In other words, the description of God evaluating creation seven times is not by coincidence. Speculative questions often come up about parallel universes and why God created this world and not another. The answer according to the way the creation account is told to us in Scripture is simply that God originally created a universe that was perfectly good. Any other world that God could have created might have been different, but not more good.

It might also be worth noting what God specifically calls "good." The following table will summarize it for us.

Table 2: The Elements of Creation God Sees as "Good"

Day	Element of creation	Evaluation
Day 1	light	good
Day 2	sky (by separating waters)	*none*, because land is the focus and pronouncing after land represents the fixed state of the three spheres of existence
Day 3	land (by separating waters)	good
Day 3	vegetation	good
Day 4	planetary bodies	good
Day 5	birds and fish	good
Day 6	animals	good
Day 6	creation of humans	*none*
Day 6	all of creation	very good

God's Goodness Is Related to His Glory

The first expression of "good" occurs after God speaks forth light on day one. In chapter 6, I suggested that the initial light in creation was intended to reflect or express the glory of God. God's glory stands as a precursor to creation and is the expression of God's character which before the fall people would have easily seen in creation. In the words of the psalmist, "The heaven's declare the glory of God; the skies proclaim the work of his hands" (Ps 19:1), and when speaking of creation, the apostle Paul says that God's eternal power and divine nature have been clearly seen from what has been made (Rom 1:20).

The creation story in Genesis 1 leaves us with only one explicit moral evaluation of creation: creation is good. If creation is an expression of God's glory, then the quality of goodness in creation is interwoven with his glory. When God sees that creation is good, he is not merely referring to the quality of his workmanship, but to his own moral quality as creator, which is seen in the end or distinct purpose given to all of creation, and the manner in which creation exists. Creation as an expression of God's glory reflects his goodness. There is no element of pre-fallen creation that exists outside the expression of God's glory and hence his goodness.

God's Goodness Is an Expression of His Providence.

A helpful way to examine the term "goodness" between the bookends of verses 3 and 31 is to investigate the term as it applies to non-living creation and living creation. Incidentally, we notice similarities to the framework created by the "it was so" expression covered in the last chapter.[2] First, the sky, seas, and land do not receive individual assessments as "good." These spheres of existence are formed by the separation of the waters, first vertically on the second day and then horizontally on the third day. Only after the land has appeared on the third day does God "see" and affirm that the land is "good." The effect is to place emphasis on the final state of the three realms that will support life, with a specific emphasis on the land which humans will occupy. Next, the planetary bodies that are created on the fourth day are also seen as "good." They provide a means by which to "separate day from the night," and "serve as signs to mark seasons and days and years." If the spheres of existence support life, the planetary bodies provide the consistent framework for the progression of life.

It is possible to overlook the meaning of God's goodness in maintaining the fixed nature of the sky, sea, and earth. Our familiarity with the inherent fixed laws of nature might prevent us from seeing these phenomena as God's expression of goodness. We discover this truth, however, when we compare the original state of creation to the events of the flood. As mentioned in the previous chapter, the flood occurs after God sees the utter corruption of people in Genesis 6:12. He decides to judge people through a flood because they have filled the earth with violence and he does this by removing the boundaries that provide the basis for life on

---

2. Although we atomize God when we talk about different aspects of his character, God holds all these qualities simultaneously.

earth to flourish. He no longer keeps the waters above the heavens separated from the waters below the heavens: " ... all the springs of the great deep burst forth, and the flood gates of the heavens were opened. And rain fell on the earth forty days and forty nights" (Gen 7:11–12).³ The flood occurs by God reversing the state of creation from its ordered state to its primordial state. There is a reversal of the stability he established on the second and third days when the waters were separated vertically and horizontally.

In this regard, the sign of the covenant—the rainbow in the sky—takes on significance. The Hebrew word for "rainbow" is the same as that for "bow," and so scholars have sometimes sought to find significance in some sort of play on words between a rainbow and a bow. But perhaps a literal understanding also derives from the word's use in this context. Noah and his descendants would look into the sky after a rainfall and see the rainbow. The rainbow in the sky would remind him that God covenanted to Noah and all living creatures to never again cut off life by the waters of a flood (Gen 9:11). The rainbow's location in the sky would testify that the sky would remain and so the floodgates of heaven would remain separated from the floodgates of the deep. The earth would continue as the "dry land" that supports life.

In a pre-fallen creation, the goodness of creation is based on the fixedness of creation, which allows for life to flourish. The establishment and continuation of the sky, earth, and sea in an orderly way is not an inherent right that humans can claim or control, but an expression of the goodness of God. Within these spheres, life flourishes and continues.

God also asserts that the living creation, the creatures that fill the three spheres of existence, is "good." What does it mean for the "hosts" or creatures that fill these spheres to be "good"? In the case of living creation, God creates all the diversity, imparts fertility, and provides sustenance for life. In regard to diversity, on the third

---

3. One of the many parallels in vocabulary between the creation story and the story of the flood is the use of the word $t^e h\hat{o}m$ ("deep") in Gen 1:2 and 7:11. In 1:2 the word describes the primordial state of the world covered by water before God speaks creation as we know it into existence.

Missing the Good God Sees in Creation

day God creates the fruit trees and vegetation, and on the fifth day he creates the aquatic life and birds, and then on the sixth day he creates all animal life according to their kind. Once again, as we mentioned in the last chapter, the phrase "according to its kind" (*lᵉ-mîn-ô*) might be better translated "every different kind"[4] and emphasizes all the diversity of life. The focus is not on colorful and detailed descriptions like Darwin gave in his *Origin of Species* and *The Descent of Man* or those we would find in a taxonomy textbook. In the Bible the focus is on God as the one who intentionally speaks forth diversity. In the case of fish and fowl, the focus is expanded to include their fullness and fecundity. God "blesses" the fish and birds to "be fruitful," "become great in number," and "fill" the earth.

A day after the affirmation of fish and fowl as good, animal life in all its diversity is also affirmed as good. The animals are not part of the blessing formula of the fish and birds, most likely because they share the realm of existence, the earth, with the humans. Since the fish and birds do not share the same sphere of existences as humans, their flourishing would not be in competition. Nevertheless, like the vegetation, fish, and birds, the animals are made according to their kind or simply God makes every different kind.

In contrast, the humans are made "male" and "female." Unlike the animals, God does not pronounce goodness on the humans after he creates them. Only after he has provided sustenance for humans and the animals does he make the pronouncement. However, like the fish and the birds, the humans are blessed to "be fruitful," "become great in number," and "fill" the earth. Noticeably different to the blessing of the fish and birds, God mandates humans "to subdue and have dominion" over all other living creatures.

The focus in creation is the expression of God's will through the command "let there be" and the declaration "and it was so," which capture God as the one who creates and sustains. The goodness in the living creation, which includes the diversity, fecundity, and purpose of all life (with humans the added element of

4. Neville, *Differentiation in Genesis*, 209–26.

purposeful rule), originates from God's command. The contrast with theories of evolution couldn't be more pronounced. Not only is God depicted as the active originator of the diversity and fecundity of life, but this diversity and fecundity is proclaimed to be "good" for this very reason.

To the question of why God created the earth, the answer is because he is good and out of his goodness he expressed his glory to create all things. These things that we often take for granted—diversity (imagine a world of sameness; some people barely tolerate eating the same breakfast two days in a row), fertility, and means to sustain ourselves—are not neutral facts that just happen to be, but express the goodness of God.

The seventh and final use of the word "good" comes when God has finished creating everything. He evaluates all of creation: "God saw all that he had made, and it was very good" (Gen 1:31). When God sees creation as good, he is communicating with us about how we are to understand the creation. He is affirming creation as good for our sake. First, the diversity is his design, not a series of random events that we are expected to believe happened in the face of statistical impossibility. Secondly, he is indicating that creation contains within it the expression of his will, which imparts to creation the potential to be bountiful and obtain the end for which he created it. That end consists of all non-living and living creation continuing in the purpose for which they have been created, as God tells us through the phrase "and it was so." This state of diversity and purpose are all part of the goodness of creation. Again, these things do not just occur naturally but are a result of the expression of God's will.

All of the above ideas—the stability and regularity of creation, the diversity of life, the imparting of fertility, and the provision of sustenance—are really describing what theologians call God's "providence." "Providence" is a word that describes how God sustains, guides, and maintains all of creation. God's providence is the personal expression of God's will in goodness to uphold all things. God's acts of creation are not neutral in and of themselves, but they are good.

One might ask, "What is the relationship between natural laws and God's providence?" What modern science describes as the laws of nature, such as gravity, fall under God's providence. Modern science describes the laws of nature as abstract principles that humans formulate from observing nature in order to describe the constancy of the world. The providence of God helps us to look at these things as the expression of God's good intention or will. From a biblical perspective, gravity is not an abstract principle the limitation of which humans should overcome to self-actualize. Rather, gravity is the framework whereby God expresses goodness to us. We don't end up floating all over the earth with everything else like objects in a spaceship. In such a floating world life could not have existed. The question we may want to ask is, why should there be gravity?

Eden a Place to Experience God's Unmitigated Goodness

At the beginning of this chapter, we noted some of the challenges in understanding parts of creation as good. We addressed this briefly as being the result of seeing creation from a human-centered perspective, which evaluates creation's goodness on its ability to serve humans in a way that brings pleasure and avoids pain. We came to conclude through the Genesis 1 text that we do indeed experience God's goodness in creation and that many of the things we take for granted are not necessarily rights we can demand. Rather, they are the intentional design of God and his sustaining of them, or his good providence.

How are we to make sense of some of the harmful natural events humans can and have experienced in creation? In the garden of Eden, Adam and Eve experienced goodness in creation as it was meant to be experienced.[5] They existed in the garden

---

5. There are those who believe the garden of Eden describes the whole world as a sacred space (Provan, *Seriously Dangerous Religion*, loc. 764). Others argue that Eden was a specific place somewhere in historical ancient Mesopotamia (Hoffmeir et. al., *Genesis*, 32–34). The approach taken here assumes

differently than when they were expelled from it. And this is the key, the initial context for humans experiencing the goodness of creation was in the context of the shelter of the garden of Eden and in direct fellowship with God.[6] In such a sheltered context we might assume that natural disasters would not have harmed the first couple.

When moral evil has entered the world via Adam and Eve's rebellion, they are expelled from the garden and their relationship with God and creation changes. Creation becomes subjected to the curse: "cursed is the ground because of you; in pain you shall eat of it all the days of your life" (Gen 3:17). Adam must now work the ground by the sweat of his brow and Eve will experience a new dimension of pain in childbirth. Adam and Eve and their descendants are no longer able to experience creation under the initial conditions of the garden of Eden. The change is also seen in the relationship with living creatures. After the flood, when God renews the original mandate to rule over creation to Noah and his sons, all living creatures are now filled with "dread" of their human rulers (Gen 9:2).

The original creation reflected God's glory in a way that has been shielded since the fall. The garden of Eden was a place where humankind lived in dependence on God. The extent and how moral evil has influenced creation has an element of mystery to it. If there were natural disasters while Adam and Eve inhabited the garden, then they were not perceived with the moral component we associate with them since the fall.

The fallen world and our part in it has influenced our experience of God's goodness in creation. We have become so dislocated from the original creation that we are unable to recognize the goodness of God in all that is there. The apostle Paul tells us that creation will be restored from its present subjugation to sin. God's love moved him to send his Son to redeem those who have subjected creation to the effects of sin. We know from the psalmist

---

Eden was a specific place.

6. For what appear to be inconsistencies in the reading of Gen 1-2, I direct the reader back to the introduction.

MISSING THE GOOD GOD SEES IN CREATION

(Ps 136) that God's steadfast love is seen in creation. However, it was the quality of his goodness expressed through his glory that he wished to display in the creation of the world in Genesis 1.

9

COMPLETE IMAGE BEARERS

We hold these truths to be self-evident, that all men are created equal, that they are endowed by their Creator with certain unalienable Rights, that among these are Life, Liberty and the pursuit of Happiness.

—FIRST LINES OF THE AMERICAN
DECLARATION OF INDEPENDENCE

IN THE FIRST SECTION of the declaration of Independence, the framers imply that there is a line, which once crossed justifies an uprising by people to overthrow their government. They justified this rebellion by appealing to the creator. Even though some of the framers were influenced by Enlightenment notions of God, they recognized that whatever rights humans had, they were given by God and these rights were fundamental to being human. People receive these rights because they are created in the image of God. In this chapter I will discuss being made in the image of God, how relating Gen 1 and 2 influences our understanding of being made in God's image, the dual nature of bearing the image of God, the nature of the first couple's commission, the triune nature in the image, and the relationship of the image to justice. Once our fundamental identity is defined, in the next chapter, we will try to understand the corruption of humanity.

One Creation in Two Accounts

Throughout church history there has been much written and debated about what it means to be created in the image of God. One example is found in the early church, where Augustine was concerned with refuting a sect called the Manicheans. They took issue with the idea that humans were created in the image of God. As Neo-Platonists, they couldn't relate any type of anthropomorphisms with the reality of God as a non-corporeal spiritual being. Their god was an abstract entity who was unable to relate to the people he had created. In contrast, in the Genesis creation story, God's act of forming Adam from the "dust" and then breathing into his nostrils the *nišmaṯ ḥayyîm* ("breath of life") expresses intimacy. God's creative Word, which represents capacity for personal relationship and is spoken by *Elohim* into his creation, now becomes the relational intimacy of *Yahweh-Elohim* forming Adam within the creation itself.

To be created in the image of God means that we are different from other physical beings like fish, birds, and animals. We are spiritual beings in a way that is similar to the way God is a spiritual being, but of course different. Nevertheless, there is a clear difference between humans and other living beings.[1] The psalmist captured this distinctiveness when he prayed, "What is man that you are mindful of him, the son of man that you care for him? You made him a little lower than the heavenly beings[2] and crowned

---

1. The distinctiveness of the creation of Adam and Eve is emphasized by the three uses of the verb *bārā'*, while it is not used to describe God's acts for any other created individual thing in Gen 1 except for the "whale" (KJV) in verse 21, which we discussed in chapter 2. Gerhard von Rad describes the creation account in Gen 1 as a pyramid, culminating with humans and in Gen 2, a concentric sphere radiating outward from man (von Rad, *Genesis*, 77).

2. The KJV has "angels." The Hebrew word is *Elohim*, which shows the range of meaning that the word *Elohim* can have. For a more detailed discussion on *Elohim*, see chapter 1.

him with glory and honor. You made him ruler over the works of your hands; you put everything under his feet..." (Ps 8:4-6).

The psalmist is describing man as he appears in the Genesis creation story.[3] In their pre-fallen state, humans reflected the glory of God and their mandate was to reflect that glory and honor God in stewarding creation. Who man is and what he does are not separated in his pre-fallen state. To speak of humans being created in the image of God describes more than just ethical qualities and capacities, such as self-giving love, holiness, creativity, et al.; and all that is revealed through the gift of speech: relational capacity, rationality, deliberation, purpose, volition, et al. To reflect the image of God, and hence his glory, is for our qualities and capacities to express themselves in our God-given mandate—to be unified people in thought, word, and deed who reflect the glory of God.[4]

What it means for humans to be created in the image of God, i.e., people as unified persons reflecting God's glory in their mandate, follows from at least three considerations. First, how one reads and therefore relates the two creation accounts of Genesis 1-2:3 and 2:4-3 can influence how one understands the image of God. Secondly, bearing the image of God relates to both humankind's qualities or capacities and function, but also dependency on God, which we will discuss in the next chapter when we talk about Adam and Eve's fall. Thirdly, the image of God can be better understood by contrasting the corruption of human nature since the fall with its eventual restoration through God's work of grace.

There are two pictures given of God creating humans in Genesis. Scholars influenced by the historical-critical method suggest that the apparent inconsistencies between the accounts point to two different creation stories, different and contradictory traditions that were passed down about creation. But before the

3. Which is probably why this psalm is a messianic psalm referring to Jesus (new Adam) in the NT and one of the reasons the writer to the Hebrews attributes these verses to Jesus (Heb 2:5-9).

4. This is the intended purpose of humankind: "... everyone who is called by my name, whom I created [*yāṣar*] for my glory [*kāvôd*], whom I formed and made" (Isa 43:7).

COMPLETE IMAGE BEARERS

rise of historical criticism this wasn't the normal way to read the text. Genesis 2 was not seen as a different creation account, but a more personal and detailed one.[5] In fact, the way the stories are recorded support reading the creation of Adam and Eve in Genesis 2 as being a more detailed part of one creation account.

To mention a few indications in the text, in Genesis 1 the words God speaks on the sixth day are ones of deliberation and intention ("let us make" not "let there be") and there is no pronouncement of finality immediately after creating the first couple ("and it was so").[6] This has the effect of leaving an openness to add more detail about the creation of humankind. In addition, Genesis 2:4 is a Janus verse[7] that connects the first part of the creation story to the more explicit details in what follows. It connects with 2:3 through the use of the Hebrew words *bārā'* (create), *yôm* (day), *'āśāh* (make), and *Elohim* (God). It points forward to Gen 2:4–25 using the *phrase 'ēlleh toledoth* ("this is the account of").[8] The strongest connection is probably through the use of the name *Yahweh-Elohim* throughout Gen 2:2–25 and not just *Yahweh* alone. Rather than emphasizing stories from different sources, these signals in the text suggest how we are to read the two accounts as one creation story. Further, seeing the creation story as a unified whole best reflects the typical form of biblical Hebrew discourse, which moves from general to specific. Genesis 1, then, tells of God creating Adam and Eve through deliberation

---

5. See for instance Umberto Cassuto's refutation of the arguments put forward from the *documentary hypothesis* (historical criticism) and his convincing arguments for seeing Gen 2 as a more personal account of Gen 1 (Cassuto, *Genesis: Part 1*, 88–100).

6. This formula breaks with its use following the previous acts of creation and will come after *Elohim* tells man that he and the beasts will have all vegetation as food. See chapter 7.

7. Janus, a Roman god with two faces, presided over the beginning and ending of conflict. A Janus verse is a transitional verse, one that looks backwards and forwards.

8. Some biblical scholars think the word *toledoth* in Gen 2:4 is a colophon (comes at the end not the beginning), so that the *toledoth* refers to Gen 1:1—2:4. However, in the other nine similar uses in the book of Genesis, it always refers to what follows.

and speech, which is given flesh through the intimate description of God forming and breathing life into Adam and then creating Eve from his side in Genesis 2.

Who Is "Adam"?

Modern scholarship has given much attention to who or what the ʾādām ("man," with the implied meaning "humankind," most translations; "human beings," NLT) in verse 26 is when God says, "Let us make ʾādām in our own image . . . " The Hebrew term ʾādām can be the proper name Adam or simply "man," or the collective noun "humankind," and by adding a vowel sound to its root one gets ʾădāmāh, the word for "earth" or "ground." For this reason and some others, some biblical scholars think the term used in Genesis 1:26 refers to an asexual being, an "earthling."[9] We can understand how "earthling" as an interpretation would be appealing in a scientifically orientated society. However, translating the word as "humankind," meaning both male and female, is the only choice that makes sense, since the word is given greater detail as male and female.

Elohim [A]   *created [bārāʾ]* [B]   ʾādām [C]
                 in his image [D]
                 in the image [D] *of*
Elohim [A¹]   *created [bārāʾ]* B]   *them* [C¹]
                 male and female [C²]
                 created [bārāʾ] [B]   *them* [C¹]

In the diagram above of Genesis 1:26, the parallel structure clearly shows the term ʾādām [C] to mean "them" [C1]. The "them" is furthered explained by the words "male and female" [C2]. Not only is this structurally discernable in the text, but it ensures that the detailed version of Eve's creation in the garden of Eden is properly understood. In Genesis 1, her creation is in reference to her being created in the image of God directly and not secondarily

---

9. Provan, *Seriously Dangerous Religion*, loc. 1611.

through Adam, even though she will be created from his side to be his "helper" (*'ēzer*) in Genesis 2. The image of male and female have their dignity or value in reflecting the glory of God through being directly related to God.

However, in the second part of the creation account, which focuses on intimate details, Adam and Eve's creation as male or female is related to the role they play as stewards of creation. In the garden, Eve's role as a "helper" (*'ēzer*) to Adam (proper name) in pre-fallen creation is emphasized. Our sinful nature has not just corrupted the ethical image of God in us, but also how we function in the mandate God has given to us. Since the church represents the living out of the future reality of creation's redemption, Paul will appeal to both creation accounts as grounds for talking about the new identity in Christ.

In Galatians, Paul talks about the new identity for those who are now in Christ, "There is neither Jew nor Greek, there is neither slave nor free, there is no male and female, for you are all one in Christ Jesus" (Gal 3:28). This is a restoring of the original image given in Genesis 1, which had been distorted through sin. In Christ, the image of God is being restored in people. Being recreated in the image of God through Christ means the collective unity and equal dignity and worth of all people in the context of diversity.

But in his instructions to Timothy, who has a charge in Ephesus, he appeals to Genesis 2 to restore order to a dysfunctional church: "I do not permit a woman to teach or to have authority over a man . . . For Adam was formed first and then Eve . . . " (1 Tim 2:11–15). The apostle Paul appeals to the order of creation of Adam and Eve in a pre-fallen world and then the order of their fall from grace.[10] He exhorts this particular church—which now becomes God's Word to all churches—to emulate the future-reality-lived-now by restoring order to their worship. The apostle does not here directly refer to Eve's role as "helper" (*'ēzer*) in the creation

---

10. But not culpability, because Adam was first issued the command not to eat from the tree of the knowledge of good and evil by God before Eve had been created.

account. Through his focus on "order," the apostle Paul might be addressing one of the ways the curse has manifested itself in Eve: "Your desire [$t^e\check{s}\hat{u}q\bar{a}h$] will be for your husband and he will rule over you." The Hebrew word for "desire" here ($t^e\check{s}\hat{u}q\bar{a}h$) also is used to describe the "desire" ($t^e\check{s}\hat{u}q\bar{a}h$) of sin that crouches at the door and devours Cain. We shouldn't' think of the word as pertaining to Eve's romantic feelings for Adam. Her desire to rule over Adam may be seen as her trying to reverse the curse of Adam's "rule" over her, symbolized in the order of creation, through her own means.

In the Genesis text, Eve's role as helper is given theological significance in the intimate relationship of marriage. In 1 Corinthians 14:33–35, Paul seems to be appealing to the notion of marriage as it derives from the creation account to speak order into the church there. Paul is most likely relating Eve's inability to overcome the effects of the curse in her own strength. Namely, the dependency of women on being delivered from the curse by means outside of themselves is probably hinted to in the last part of the apostle's phrase in the 2 Timothy text: " . . . But women will be saved through childbearing—if they continue in faith, love and holiness with propriety."[11]

As we move into entrenched post-Christian societies, the world has exerted an undue influence on the roles of women and men in the church. Nevertheless, the oppression and exploitation of women exposes the reality that sin has corrupted not only our nature, but how we perceive our roles in families and the church. The renewal of creation and the people of God are occurring through Christ and so the restoration of the corrupted image, including the role of both men and women, is being renewed through Christ in the church.

Our understanding of our image and how we belong in God's plan of restoration is related to a proper knowledge of God. When we lack proper knowledge of God, our understanding of creation

---

11. To delve into a deeper exegesis of this text is beyond the scope here. The main point is that the apostle appeals to the creation texts (Adam and Eve) to establish order in the church and the modern church must wrestle with the meaning of these texts.

becomes distorted and so does our place within it. We start to think independently of God. Creation, including ourselves, becomes something we can manipulate according to our own desires and wishes. But, as we will see in the next chapter, these desires are not always reliable guides. The outcome is the distortion of our ability to perceive our gender roles in creation distinctly as man or woman. Our natures become corrupted to the point that God allows us to go our own way and pursue our autonomy in sexual expression. Rather than being a new form of liberation, it reflects deep despair that goes back to the most primitive times (Rom 1).

The New Mandate

The view that the image of God in Genesis refers to humankind as rulers in the place of God is as early as John Chrysostom, one of the early church fathers.[12] The Reformer Calvin did not agree with the idea proposed by Chrysostom and popular today that the image of God lies in humankind's act as vice-regent in the government of this world.[13] He would say that being created in the image of God has more to do with who humans are than the fulfillment of a mandate. Calvin makes a valid point, but in the giving of the mandate there are also clues as to what it means to be created in the image of God. In a sinless world, God's mandate "to have dominion over all creatures" (Gen 1:26) involves "working" the garden of Eden and "keeping" it (Gen 2:15).

Adam and Eve derive their authority to rule from the mandate given to them. "To subdue or rule" carries for the modern reader nuances of exploitation, which after the fall has become the reality. But we shouldn't think of the mandate as encouraging a degrading of creation any more than to think that people would

---

12. In the ANE environment, it was often common for the king to be thought of as the image or representative of his god on earth. So, the king of Babylon was the son of Marduk, the patron god of Babylon. And when King Nabonidus replaced Marduk with Sîn, his moon god, according to the priests of Marduk at the time, his throne was usurped from him by Cyrus the Great.

13. Calvin, *Genesis*, 75.

go home after work and trash their own homes. Most people take care of their homes. Subduing and ruling have a positive connotation if God is good and loving. Adam and Eve's rule in a sinless world would have been as beneficial as if God had ruled it himself. The referent point of God's kingship or rule over creation gives meaning to humankind's kingship. Without this referent point, we can never determine the ends of creation. God's kingship provides morality, meaning, and purpose to creation.[14]

For humans, the call to "have dominion over the fish of the sea and over the birds of the heavens and over every living thing that moves on the earth" (Gen 1:28, ESV) is preceded by the blessing, "Be fruitful and multiply and fill the earth." Both the mandate and the blessing are given as commands. Yet, to understand the full nature of this blessing, we have to understand it as pertaining to pre-fallen humankind.

The command to be fruitful and multiply and fill the earth takes on a different nuance for Adam and Eve after they have fallen from grace. The ground becomes cursed, as do the relationships that will mark the first family and hence all families that follow. Cain will murder Abel. Sin will become a powerful force, which is described as "crouching at the door" (Gen 4:7), ready to pounce, and as something people cannot "rule over." Humanity spreads out from the garden and becomes progressively violent and lustful. God intercedes and brings about the judgment of the flood. Noah and his family are kept safe from the flood by taking refuge in an ark he patiently built over decades. After the flood, when Noah steps on dry ground again, God "blesses" Noah and his sons and commands them "to be fruitful and multiply and fill the earth." But instead of ruling peacefully over the fish, birds, and animals, "The fear and dread" of humankind will fall on all living creatures of the earth (Gen 9:2).

As God continues in his plan to redeem humankind, the command takes the form of blessing on the Mesopotamian Abraham: "I will make you into a great nation, and I will bless you; I will make your name great, and you will be a blessing. I will

---

14. Houston, *I Believe*, 44–49.

bless those who bless you, and whoever curses you I will curse; and all peoples on earth will be blessed through you" (Gen 12:2–3). Ancient Israel became the heirs of these promises. The exile of the Northern Kingdom in 722 by the Assyrians and Judah in 586 by the Babylonians brought an end to their literal fulfilment.

Finally reaching Jesus, the mandate became a spiritual principal. The original mandate to rule is given in a tri-formulaic fashion—rule, multiply, and fill. Jesus' tri-formulaic command to his disciples is to go and make disciples of all nations, baptizing them in the name of the Father, Son, and Holy Spirit (Matt 28:18–20). Jesus brought to actualization what the prophets had begun to proclaim, that the original mandate to rule over creation cannot be separated from a moral framework that involves submission to God the Father and the restoration of the fallen image. Likewise, the apostle Paul writes about the close relationship of creation to the salvation of people: "For the creation waits with eager longing for the revealing of the sons of God" (Rom 8:19).

This is not to suggest that we should be any less excellent stewards of creation and not be concerned about modern environmental concerns, but to recognize that Adam and Eve's mandate was not merely "secular" as we might be influenced to see it today. There was a holistic understanding of the world and humankind's place in the world. The vital spiritual dimension was decoupled because of sin. True stewardship of creation involved a holistic rule where the image of God in humans reflecting the character of God is in harmony with the mandate of God. This complete picture would reflect the glory of God.

Jesus as the Word of creation would set in motion the healing of the broken image, both in the forgiveness of sins and the restoration of the whole person and the true mandate. If God so loved the world that he sent his one and only son to save the world, then we can only imagine that the gift of creation was also an expression of not only his goodness but his steadfast love. The psalmist captures this in Psalm 136.

The "seed" that was narrowed down to one family in Abraham and then multiplied to become ancient Israel would once again be narrowed down and find its fulfillment in Jesus Christ, Abraham's "seed" (Gal 3:15). His seed would then multiply to become the spiritual seed, the church, where in Christ there is neither Jew nor Greek, slave nor free, male nor female, but all are one in Christ Jesus (Gal 3:28). The heirs of Abraham would be those who believe by faith (Gal 3:7).

The Word as a Clue to What Being Created in the Image of God Means

To be created in the image of God also means to reflect the triune nature of God. What is meant when *Elohim* says, "Let us make *adam* in our own image..."? The plural allows for different interpretations: a plural of majesty, the heavenly council, or the triune nature of God. Christians hold that the natural reading is to refer to the triune nature of God for several good reasons. The terms ṣelem ("image") and dᵉmût ("likeness") used in Genesis 1:26 are also used of Adam having a son, Seth, in his own ṣelem ("image") and dᵉmût ("likeness"; Gen 5:3). Seth is made in the specific sense of Adam, not in the general sense of humankind. Further, interpreting the plural as referring to the "heavenly council" of beings greatly limits what it means to be human. What would it mean to be created in the image of a "heavenly council"? Certainly, being created in the image of God has more to do with just having a spiritual nature.

The pre-fallen nature of God is given in his triune glory in Genesis 1:1: Father, Word, and Spirit. The triune nature of God explains the social nature of humankind, the capacity for love and particularly the unique relationship between Adam and Eve. In the New Testament, the doctrine of the image of God is closely tied up with God the Son, not with angels, who belong in a heavenly council. "The Son is the radiance of God's glory and the exact representation of his being, sustaining all things by his powerful word" (Heb 1:3). "And we all, who with unveiled faces contemplate the Lord's glory, are being transformed into his image with ever-increasing glory, which comes from the Lord, who is the Spirit" (2

Cor 3:18). We are being transformed into the likeness of Christ. As we become conformed to Christ's likeness, we are becoming image bearers. We are granted the status of coheirs with Christ (Rom 8:17), those who will eventually judge the angels (1 Cor 6:3).

The Problem of Pursuing Justice Outside of People Bearing the Image of God

Lastly, as stewards emulating the rule of the king, the notion of justice is tied into bearing the image of God. In Isaiah 3:15 we read, "'What do you mean by crushing my people, by grinding the face of the poor?' declares the Lord GOD of hosts." This is obviously a metaphor relating oppression to the destroying of the image of God. The idea of grinding faces captures explicitly how injustice is related to the de-imaging of people.

To return to the beginning of this chapter, the framers of the American Constitution struggled with a tension. They understood the importance of submitting to authorities. So, it was only after all attempts, in their eyes, to petition King George III with their grievances had failed that they unilaterally declared independence from England. Importantly, the wrongdoings they felt were assessed according to the rights each person had been given by their creator.

They stood in contrast with many of the twentieth-century movements that pursued justice on a generic basis. These groups approached the issue of injustice not in relationship to the image of God, but through social class, of which people were assigned usually to one of two classes. The classes were divided into the owners of the means of production and the workers (so Engels and Marx) or, in a different, more modern variation, these groups can be race based. Class or race, rather than the image of God, becomes the lens by which to understand a person and oppression.

The road to hell is paved with good intentions, so the saying goes. The twentieth-century movements began by rightly acknowledging inequalities that were harmful to certain groups of people. However, their demand for justice approached people abstractly and through stereotype. The history of these movements has shown that the oppressed often rise up to become the new oppressors, and in a way more demeaning to humanity. The reason for this is their inability to recognize that the oppressed have as corrupt a nature as the oppressor. The difference between the two groups is that the oppressed are not in a place where absolute power can corrupt absolutely. History has also shown that these movements move towards totalitarian regimes, so that absolute power can be secured absolutely. Only in the notion of each individual created as a unique image bearer of God can the roots of oppression be properly understood and addressed. We will explore the corrupted nature of humankind in the next chapter.

10

THE CORRUPTION OF HUMANITY

For just as through the disobedience of the one man the many were made sinners, so also through the obedience of the one man the many will be made righteous.

—ROM 5:19

ONE OF THE THEMES of this book has been how the sinfulness of humankind has in some way affected all of creation. There is such a complex web of cause and effect that we aren't always sure how sin displays itself in the brokenness of the world, including people. For example, the proper physical wiring of our brains can make the difference between a life that seems smooth and transitions from success to success and a life simmering with frustration and lack of focus. One doctor tells us that people with attention deficit disorder (ADD) have brains where the neuronal connections in the cortex do not develop in a normal pattern. As a result, the frontal cortex, which controls emotions and impulse, becomes improperly regulated. The untreated child begins his or her school life unable to concentrate. As time goes by, the child becomes less enthusiastic about any type of studying and eventually falls behind. These children often can lack impulse control. They become caught in a negative cycle where the outcome tends to be insurmountable educational challenges and social alienation. It doesn't mean that children with ADD can't be successful. Some people with ADD can go on to become quite successful.

Gabor Maté, the doctor mentioned above, is one such person. He wrote the national bestseller about ADD called *Scattered Minds*. He believes that it is our environment, especially our interactions with our primary caregivers, that can lead to uneven wiring in our brains. But he's not completely sure. He describes his own struggle with ADD as having roots in the horrific persecution of the Jews in Europe during WWII, the atrocities of which his family experienced firsthand.

But are we responsible for our moral choices, or are we victims who have no control over what Mother Nature has dealt us?[1] Are we just innocent victims whose mantra is a line from a pop song—"I was born this way"? Pastor Rick Warren,[2] known as "America's pastor," was asked on a *HuffPost* live interview about what he had said on a Piers Morgan interview:

> So you think it is possible that people are born with a natural desire, but still it would be a sin. God would create a situation whereby people could have feelings and desires which are natural to them and it's still a sin?

During the question, Pastor Warren responds with "I think so." And when the question is over, he answers, "I do not have it all figured out. But I do know that I am called to love everybody."[3]

Original Sin

Of course, Pastor Warren was talking about an issue that has resulted in serious division in Western mainline churches. The

---

1. I am not referring here to the incapacitating and devastating effects of mental illness. Rather I am talking about defending moral choices on a purely naturalistic basis.

2. Pastor and author of the *New York Times* number-one bestseller *The Purpose Driven Life*.

3. Retrieved from https://www.youtube.com/watch?v=03Z5C1nxCJI.

generality of the language, though, could describe anything that involves going against one's apparently natural desires, when there is a contradiction with God's Word.

To understand the unreliability of some of these natural desires, we need to understand the fundamental nature that each person has inherited since the fall. Theologians refer to this nature as "original sin," a term made popular by Augustine. It is the corrupted nature that all people have inherited as a result of Adam and Eve's willful disobedience of God. King David summarizes what original sin is in his prayer of repentance. He had taken Bathsheba in adultery and tried covering up his deed by having her husband, Uriah, killed in battle. When he was confronted by Nathan the prophet, David remorsefully cried out, "Behold, I was brought forth in iniquity, and in sin did my mother conceive me" (Ps 51:5).

The Condition of Dependency and Freedom to Be Truly Human

Reflecting the glory of God as image bearers before the fall was the natural state for Adam and Eve. They lived as individuals and as a couple in holistic well-being (*shalom*) with God. Their thoughts, words, and deeds were unified reflecting that their wills were in line with how they perceived reality.

Adam and Eve were created with the capacity to choose, that is, to exercise their wills. We would be in error, though, if we thought that being created with the capacity to choose meant the ability to do absolutely anything. Adam and Eve could only reflect God's glory by living dependently on God. This is the significance of the LORD-God's command to Adam, "You are free to eat from any tree in the garden; but you must not eat from the tree of the knowledge of good and evil, for when you eat from it you will certainly die" (Gen 3:16-17). Adam and Eve were always meant to make choices in the context of relating to God by obeying his command.

God alone has the capacity for absolute freedom. All other created beings derive their freedom as a gift from him. The core of this freedom is the freedom to love, which is reflected in the very nature of the triune God. The command to Adam and Eve seems prohibitive, but its purpose was to create the context whereby, deriving their freedom from God, they could truly love and live life in fullness as image bearers.

In the garden, Adam and Eve have the choice to express their autonomy from God in one matter. The trees of the garden were "pleasant to the sight and good for food" (Gen 2:9). Only one tree and one command not to eat of it sets the parameters for understanding their dependency on God. At this point their wills naturally incline to make choices in accordance with God's command, i.e., to live in dependence on him.

Their dependency is challenged by the serpent. We shouldn't think of this serpent as an aetiological myth (an untrue story that explains the origins of something) and that Moses was passing on folklore that might be amusing to an ophiologist. We are told the adversary came to Eve in the form of a serpent, craftier than all the other "animals of the field,"[4] which is consistent with the creation account in Genesis 1–2 focusing on the concrete reality of the world that we live in. Only after sin has entered into the world do we see supernatural beings, "cherubim," guarding the garden of Eden. Only in Genesis 6 with the "sons of God" taking the daughters of men as they pleased does the biblical story hint at spiritual boundaries transgressing physical boundaries.[5] Furthermore, the only other instance of an animal speaking in the Bible is Balaam's donkey in Numbers 22:21–40. In this story, we are shown

---

4. The traditional interpretation has been that the serpent is a manifestation of Satan. Some scholars say that there is nothing in the OT that suggests the serpent is Satan and perhaps only Rom 16:20 in the New Testament. However, where else could this source of evil which was in antithesis to God come from? Who or what would have the nature and audacity to challenge God's command?

5. The first sin appears to have consequences that touched reality seen and unseen.

the spiritual realm, something Balaam does not see. We are also told the donkey speaks because the LORD "opened the donkey's mouth."

The adversary manipulates the divine gift of speech to tempt Eve. Speech is something that humans alone share with God. God blesses all living creatures, but to the humans, "He says to them" (Gen 2:8) in giving them their commission, and he tells them, "Behold, I give to you . . . " (Gen 2:9) in providing their sustenance. Not even when God curses the serpent does he enter into dialog with it, like he does with Adam and Eve. The adversary's form of a serpent is symbolic of his *modus operandi*—deception. The "heel"[6] that would crush his skull implies he was a deceiver from the beginning (John 8:43–45).

A New Reality

The temptation Eve faces centers around her particular reality, which was framed by God's command not to eat of the tree of the knowledge of good and evil.[7] Adam and Eve were meant to experience the fullness of life by living according to the command of the LORD. To live in dependency on God is to live a life of faith. In other words, Eve's temptation was really a test of faith. The adversary is able to get Eve to look at the act of eating the fruit from a perspective that removes the authenticity of God's command. He first gets her to question the existence of the command, "Did God really say . . . " (v. 2), then the certainty of the command, "You will not surely die . . . " (v. 4). He then changes the consequence of the one prohibition, "you will surely die," to " . . . your eyes will be opened and you will be like God, knowing good and evil" (v. 5). The command was given to provide the conditions necessary for dependency and hence true humanity. The serpent gets Eve

---

6. The Hebrew word for "heel" (*yakēv*) has the same root letters and sounds similar to the adjective in Hebrew "deceitful" (*yakōv*).

7. There have been various proposals made about what the "knowledge" of good and evil is. In 2 *Baruch* 56:6–10, the suggestion is sexual knowledge. Philo believed it was physical pleasures (Provan, *Dangerous Religion*, 73).

to look at reality from outside of God's command. The tree of the knowledge of good and evil bore fruit that was pleasing to the eye, like all the trees in the garden. The tree remains constant. It is only in this alternative view of reality that Eve can choose to know good or evil independently of God's command.

Through the reality projected by the serpent, the command became something it was never meant to be, "prohibition to fulfillment." Adam and Eve were created in perfection as image bearers. Ironically, their complete fulfillment as God intended occurred only as long as they obeyed the command. The breaching of the command would unleash the altered reality of "death" and "curse." Deceived by the adversary, Eve now perceives the fruit as "desirable for gaining wisdom." She takes and eats of the fruit and gives some to Adam, who eats it as well. Since Adam was first issued the command not to eat of the tree of the knowledge of good and evil before Eve was created, he had also neglected his duty to exercise appropriate rule over the earth. Had he fulfilled his role, he would have rebuked the serpent.

Humankind was never created to have moral autonomy, i.e., to choose what is good and evil by themselves. This prerogative belongs to God alone. When Adam and Eve lived in dependence on God, they naturally reflected God's character as image bearers. Their new form of knowing good and evil completely changed Adam and Eve's nature. Furthermore, this new distorted way of perceiving reality became fixed in their natures. They were no longer able to see each other as image bearers of God. Their differences as male and female were something to be ashamed of. They now must cover themselves with fig leaves, a form of hiding from one another. They can no longer naturally interact transparently in the distinctiveness of who they were created to be.

More so, their relationship with God has become altered. They now wish to hide from God, whereas before their act of defiance, they regularly walked with him in the garden. God's very presence confronts Adam and Eve with their disobedience. Adam and Eve now perceive of themselves through the lens of despair

The Corruption of Humanity

and they are unable to stand transparently before their creator.[8] All desires that lead people to turn away from God are those that originate out of this despair. True knowledge can only come by standing transparently before God. Adam and Eve take the opposite posture by hiding from God. Their choice has created a new form of existence. They no longer live according to the command of God and their fundamental nature becomes altered. They now hide from each other and God. Their new state of existence is one that is described by shame and fear.

This corrupted nature has been passed on to the rest of humanity. Ironically, people have no problem understanding shared physical traits with one's ancestors, but this spiritual connection is difficult to understand. However, we are not culpable as sinners because we have inherited this nature, but we are culpable as sinners because of our willful actualization of it. Our natures are such that, like Adam and Eve, we turn away from God and others, to ourselves.[9] Men loved darkness instead of light, John tells us (John 3:9).

It's only when Eve exercises her free will outside of God's command that she loses her free will. It seems ironic, but humans are no longer able to exercise their free will in dependence on God and hence have lost the ability to reflect God's glory. The apostle Paul wrote, "the god of this world has blinded the minds of the unbelievers, to keep them from seeing the light of the gospel of the glory of Christ, who is the image of God" (2 Cor 4:4). Rather than making willful choices, people have lost their ability to choose as God had originally endowed the first couple.

Jesus' refutation of Satan in Matthew 4:4 and Luke 4:4 becomes important because he addresses the fundamental issue of what it means to be truly human. To be human at its most fundamental level is to live according to the Word of God. In Luke's telling of

---

8. As Soren Kirkegaard describes our spiritual state before coming to faith in Christ in his work *Sickness unto Death*.

9. Hence, the greatest commandment is to "Love the Lord your God with all your heart and with all your soul and with all your mind" and the second is to "love your neighbor as yourself" (Matt 22:38–39).

Jesus' life, he places the temptation of Jesus after he is baptized, which symbolizes the start of his public ministry. Then Luke traces Jesus' genealogy to Adam rather than to Abraham as Matthew does in his gospel. Some biblical scholars suggest this is because Luke was writing for a Gentile rather than Jewish audience. However, the story of Jesus successfully rebuking Satan contrasts with Adam and Eve's failure to do so. Jesus restored in his life what the life of dependency was meant to look like: "For I have come down from heaven, not to do my own will but the will of him who sent me" (John 6:38).

When we talk about our natural desires and feelings, we cannot be sure whether they are the result of the brokenness of the world and the nature we have inherited. They may be symptoms of a greater despair that each person experiences as a result of original sin. We can only truly gauge these feelings in the context of the command of God. This command finds its fullest expression in the life, death and resurrection of Jesus, where "no" becomes a "yes" (2 Cor 1:20). To stand transparently before God is to surrender to Jesus the Messiah, who undoes the effects of sin. For as sin entered the world through Adam, how much more did the gift and God's grace come through Jesus Christ (Rom 5:12, 15). The writer to Hebrews tells us, "the word of God is living and active, sharper than any two-edged sword, piercing to the division of soul and of spirit, of joints and of marrow, and discerning the thoughts and intentions of the heart" (Heb 4:12). The apostle John tells us, Jesus is the Word of God (John 1:1–3). The image of God safeguarded by the original command is once again restored through him.

11

ENTERING INTO SABBATH REST

> So God blessed the *seventh day* and made it holy, because on it God rested from all his work that he had done in creation.
>
> —GEN 2:3, ESV

THE SCOTT ERIC LIDDLE was favored to win the gold medal in the one-hundred-meter sprint at the 1924 Paris Olympics, but forfeited running the race because it was to be held on Sunday, the Christian Sabbath. Interestingly, Harold Abrahams, his Jewish English teammate, won the race. Their stories were popularized in the Hollywood movie *Chariots of Fire*.

Many Millennials and Generation Z-ers would find it hard to relate to Liddle's world. But the keeping the Sabbath formed an important part of life in many Western countries. Canada had a centuries-old law, the Lord's Day Act,[1] which banned shopping on Sunday. In 1985 the act was overturned by the supreme court in a case brought by Big M Drug Mart. The Canadian constitution had just been patriated from England in 1982 and a new Canadian Charter of Rights and Freedoms had been added.

---

1. The Canadian version instituted in 1906 was a derivative from the English law passed in the seventeenth century during the time of Charles I.

Contours of Creation

Unknown to many Canadians, the former well-known Eaton Center in downtown Toronto, named after its founder, Timothy Eaton, at one time had the blinds drawn on Sundays so that people would not even window shop.[2] For many people today it would be hard to relate to this type of observance. The truth is that in many Western societies the concept of resting on the Sabbath had an important role.

If we were to write out the words from Genesis 2:1–3 as they occur in the Hebrew, to show its structure, we would get the following.[3]

[1] The Heavens and Earth were finished [kālāh] and all their hosts.

[2] God finished [kālāh] seventh day his works [mᵉlāḵᵓāʰ] which he did [ʿāśāh]
[He] rested [šāḇaṯ] seventh day his works [mᵉlāḵᵓāʰ] which he did [ʿāśāh]
[3] God blessed seventh day
God holy-ed it
FOR on it
(He) rested [šāḇaṯ]   his works [mᵉlāḵᵓāʰ] which created [bārāʾ]
                                                            God
                                                                  did [ʿāśāh]

We are told that on the seventh day God rested from his works[4] which he made.[5] Each of the words "seventh," "works," and "made" are used three times for emphasis and add cohesion

---

2. This story was related to me by Vincent Craven, who while serving in the Australian army in WWII contracted malaria and came to the much cooler climate of Canada to lead IVCF and Pioneer Camp Ministries.

3. I have left out some phrases and used the Hebrew order of the words to show the carefully composed literary repetition in the Hebrew. Later these words would be use in describing building the temple. Some scholars have pointed out that the language God uses to describe his rest is often used with work related to the priestly service, or the building of the tabernacle. So, for example we read, "their brothers the Levites helped them, until the work [mᵉlāḵᵓāʰ] was finished [kālāh]—for the Levites were more upright in heart than the priests in consecrating themselves" (2 Chr 29:34). This would certainly reinforce the "holiness" of the seventh day.

4. mᵉlāḵᵓāʰ.

5. ʿāśāh.

to these verses. To emphasize that what God made he alone had created (and to form an *inlusio* with 1:1), Moses awkwardly has the verb "created" (*bārāʾ*) followed by the infinitive form of the verb "made." English translations smooth this out to "... he had done in creation" (Gen 2:3).

From the way the verses are written, the emphasis is placed on God blessing and making holy the seventh day. The statement "God rested" comes before and immediately after the statement "God blessed the seventh day and made it holy." The passage sets the context of God resting with making the day holy and blessing it. Moses even uses the coordinating conjunction "for," which indicates the reason.

The sacredness of the seventh day derives its meaning in relation to the work God has done in creation. God blesses and makes holy the seventh day because he has finished his work. The term "blessing" means to give something the capacity to flourish as God had intended. So, after he has created the fish and birds he blesses them, and after he creates the humans and given them their mandate to rule creation he blesses them. Blessing in this regard signifies that creation was to continue in its completed state and exist in this perfect state perpetually. The other term, "holy-ed," refers to the holiness of creation, which is the goodness and glory of God reflected in creation. This state of holiness and blessing was reflected in God's completed work.

The seventh day represents the final intended state of everything. Whether Adam and Eve in a pre-fallen world would have observed the Sabbath is debated by theologians. Most likely, they entered into a rest in the garden that was perpetual, like the one the author to Hebrews mentions,[6] until they were expelled for disobedience. The Sabbath as a command is only given to God's people after the great act of deliverance from Egypt. Nevertheless, the Sabbath was part of the original created order. People keep the Sabbath as a recurring phenomenon. In contrast, God's Sabbath is a one-time observance. In the original creation there was no day after the Sabbath for God to get back to work. Jesus will note in

---

6. See below.

Mark 2:27 this important principal, that the Sabbath was created for humankind, not the other way around.

When we turn to the Ten Commandments, we see that the reason for Sabbath keeping is related to God's model in creation: "Remember the Sabbath day, to keep it holy... For in six days the LORD made heaven and earth, the sea, and all that is in them, and rested on the seventh day. Therefore the LORD blessed the Sabbath day and made it holy" (Exod 20:8, 11). But as we know from the second set of commandments Moses gives to the Israelites in Deuteronomy 5, also because of their redemption, "You shall remember that you were a slave in the land of Egypt, and the LORD your God brought you out from there with a mighty hand and an outstretched arm. Therefore, the LORD your God commanded you to keep the Sabbath day" (Deut 5:15). These concepts may seem to be unrelated, but they really aren't. The Sabbath rest represents the created order as God had intended it before Adam and Eve disobeyed. God's deliverance is part of the process of God working to restore that original order.

The restoration of creation is not thought of independently from the restoration of the image of God in humankind. This is the link between the two different reasons for keeping the Sabbath. The New Testament interprets the redemption of humanity through Christ and so his resurrection day became the new Sabbath.[7] The resurrected Christ represents the overcoming of death and decay and the new life that was part of the original creation, a life once again reflecting the glory of God. The writer to Hebrews will explain this new reality as the new state of rest for the Christian. To enter into relationship with Christ becomes the rest that God had originally intended and so is equated with God's resting: "So then, there remains a Sabbath rest for the people of God, for whoever has entered God's rest has also rested from his works as God did from his" (Heb 4:9–10).

---

7. "Now on *the first day* of the week... Then the other disciple, who had reached the tomb first, also went in, and he saw and believed; for as yet they did not understand the Scripture, that he must rise from the dead" (John 20:1, 8, 9). See also Acts 20:7.

Entering into Sabbath Rest

But there has always lingered, with the ancients as well as the moderns, the question as to what regulations from the Torah needed to be followed. A sizeable oral tradition had developed in Judaism before Jesus' time and could be seen in the likes of the Pharisees' attitudes to his activities on the Sabbath.[8] Jesus claimed that "the Sabbath was made for man, not man for the Sabbath. So the Son of Man is Lord even of the Sabbath" (Mark 2:24–28).

The Christian observance of the Sabbath follows along the lines of celebrating entering into rest through Jesus' death and resurrection. This Sabbath celebration remembers the holiness of creation and the redemption of people. Christians who celebrate on Sunday have good grounds. They are remembering the holiness of God's creation—that he created everything purposefully and placed people in it out of his goodness; that the restoration of creation would ultimately come through the means of human redemption in Christ; that on the first day of the week Christ arose from the grave and so defeated death. Christ is celebrated in the gathering of Christians to worship on the Sabbath.

We live in post-Christian societies where the concept of Sabbath is confused with a day off from work, even among Christians. In former times, the Sabbath was a time of worship, which would necessitate a taking off a good portion of the day. Not having any obligations allowed Christians to worship and fellowship together and to be involved in restorative events with family and friends and other believers, even to extend acts of mercy. The focus is not on achieving results but living out the rest we have entered into as a foretaste of the rest that is to come. Such rest is not idleness, but an envisaging of the process of re-creation and redemption in anticipation of Christ's return. The problem is that we are losing the ability to choose how we will keep Sabbath. In our increasingly post-Christian societies, we will need to learn how to practice the rest we have already entered into in Christ. We will need to learn to practice eternity more creatively and actively.

---

8. They criticized his disciples picking grain to eat (Luke 6:1–2) and his healing on the Sabbath (Mark 2:24–28).

12

SOME FINAL THOUGHTS

WE BEGAN OUR JOURNEY by noting that creation plays a more central role in our lives than might be recognized at first. God as the creator and his claim on all his creation has been challenged through the social-intellectual environment that came out of the Enlightenment. In particular, the biblical witness has come to be seen as an unreliable guide. The result has been a lack of confidence in the biblical creation account as the Word of God. The effect, though, has larger implications. If the first several chapters in the Bible lack trustworthiness and truthfulness, then what about the rest of the Bible? People are less likely to engage in something they are uncertain about and so they withdraw from biblical study and other spiritual disciplines. Ironically, as they do, they withdraw from communicating with God, whose Word at creation speaks of his desire for relationship with people, whom he has created.

I have argued that the biblical tradition is no more unreasonable than any other ideology that tries to make sense of our world. The difference is that it requires a faith commitment, which is a belief that there is a God and that the Bible truthfully and trustworthily bears witness to God, creation, and ourselves. We also recognized that the creation stories were given to us in a particular genre and their interpretation requires a sensitivity to the genre of the biblical texts. However, genre does not determine whether events actually occurred, only how we are to interpret them.

Some Final Thoughts

Our journey in reading the biblical creation story began by noticing what the initial condition of creation tells us about the reality of existence. God exists in a triune nature, and this is the picture we see before sin has entered into the world. Creation itself is an expression of God's will through his Word. There is no other reality of existence in the biblical worldview. All of creation serves the purpose it was created for, including darkness, which is expelled by the glory of God's light. Creation is an expression of God's glory.

We explored the trustworthiness of God's Word, its certainty that "it was so," and how this trait is reflected in creation. We also looked at the diversity and continued sustenance of creation and how these attributes reflect God's goodness. Humans, we noted, were the crown of creation, created to reflect God's glory through their lives individually, in relationship, and in the stewarding of creation. Love necessitated the creation of humans with free will.

However, the gift of speech was manipulated by Satan, the adversary, to cause Eve to see reality in a way it was never meant to be seen, apart from dependency on God. Adam and Eve's choice to listen to the serpent and disobey God destined themselves, their descendants, and the whole human race to alienation from God—to despair. The biblical story of God's steadfast love in redeeming people begins here and culminates in Jesus Christ, who is the true Word. When we enter into relationship with God through Christ, we enter into the rest that is the culmination of God's work in creation. When we embrace God's Word, we begin the process of the restoration of our humanity—the image of God—until the day "we shall be like him, for we shall see him as he is" (1 John 3:2).

Bibliography

Allen, Reginald E., ed. *Greek Philosophy: Thales to Aristotle.* 3rd ed. New York: Free Press, 1991.

Augustine, *On Genesis: Two Books on Genesis: Against the Manichees and On the Literal Interpretation of Genesis: An Unfinished Book.* Translated by Roland J. Teske. Washington, DC: Catholic University of America Press, 1991.

Barth, Karl. *Church Dogmatics* II.1, *The Doctrine of God.* Translated by T. H. L. Parker et al. Edinburgh: T. & T. Clark, 1957.

Brueggemann, Walter. *Genesis.* Interpretation: A Bible Commentary for Teaching and Preaching. Louisville: Westminster John Knox, 1982.

Buber, Martin. *I and Thou.* Translated by Walter Kaufmann. New York: Scribner, 1970.

Calvin, John. *Commentaries on the First Book of Moses Called Genesis.* Translated by Rev. John King. Grand Rapids: Christian Classics Ethereal Library, n.d.

Cassuto, Umberto. *A Commentary on the Book of Genesis: Part One, From Adam to Noah.* Translated by Israel Abrahams. Skokie, IL.: Varda, 1989.

Childs, Brevard. *Introduction to Old Testament as Scripture.* Philadelphia: Fortress, 1979.

Curtis, Adrian. *Ugarit Ras Shamra: Cities of the Biblical World.* Grand Rapids: Eerdmans, 1985.

Dalley, Stephanie. *Myths from Mesopotamia.* Translated by Stephanie Dalley. Rev. ed. Oxford World's Classics. Oxford: Oxford University Press, 1989.

———. *Myths from Mesopotamia: Creation, the Flood, Gilgamesh, and Others.* Oxford: Oxford University Press, 2000.

Darwin, Charles. *The Descent of Man, and Selection in Relation to Sex.* 2nd ed. New York: Appleton, 1874.

———. *The Origin of Species by Means of Natural Selection or the Preservation of Favoured Races in the Struggle for Life.* 6th ed. London: John Murray, 1872.

Durant, Will. *The Story of Philosophy.* New York: Pocket Books, 1961.

BIBLIOGRAPHY

Earhart, H. Byron. *Religion in the Japanese Experience: Sources and Interpretations.* The Religious Life of Man. Belmont, CA: Wadsworth, 1974.

Fee, Gordon. *Paul the Spirit and the People of God.* Grand Rapids: Baker, 1996.

Fout, Jason A. *The Glory of God and the Human Creature in Karl Barth, Hans Urs von Balthasar and Theological Exegesis of Scripture.* New York: Bloomsbury T. & T. Clark, 2015.

Gay, Peter. *The Enlightenment an Interpretation: The Rise of Modern Paganism.* New York: Norton, 1966.

Grisanti, Michael. "Old Testament Poetry as a Vehicle for Historiography." *Bibliotheca Sacra* (2004) 172–77.

Harris, R. Laird, et al. *The Theological Wordbook of the Old Testament.* Chicago: Moody, 1980.

Hasel, Gerhard F. "The Problem of History in Old Testament Theology." *Andrews University Seminary Studies* 8.1 (1970) 23–50.

Himmelfarb, Gertrude. *The Roads to Modernity: The British, French, and American Enlightenments.* New York: Vintage, 2004.

Hoffmeir, James, et al. *Genesis: History, Fiction, or Neither.* Counterpoints Series. Grand Rapids: Zondervan, 2015.

Houston, James. *I Believe in the Creator.* London: Hodder and Stoughton, 1979.

Kierkegaard, Soren. *The Sickness unto Death: A Christian Psychological Exposition for Edification and Awakening by Anti-Climacus.* London: Penguin, 1989.

Konig, Ed. "The Latest Phase of the Controversy Over Babylon and the Bible." *American Journal of Theolog* 9.3 (July 1905).

Maté, Gabor. *Scattered Minds: A New Look at the Origins and Healing of Attention Deficit Disorder.* Toronto: Vintage Canada, 1999.

"Mathematical Challenges to Darwin's Theory of Evolution." *Uncommon Knowledge* with Peter Robinson. Interview with David Berlinski, Stephen C. Meyer, David H. Gelernter. Hoover Institution, July 22, 2019. https://www.hoover.org/research/mathematical-challenges-darwins-theory-evolution-david-berlinski-stephen-meyer-and-david.

Moran, William L. *The Amarna Letters.* Baltimore: Johns Hopkins University Press, 1992.

Neville, Richard. "Differentiation in Genesis 1: An Exegetical Creation *Ex Nihilo.*" *Journal of Biblical Literature* 130.2 (2011) 209–26.

Niebuhr, Reinhold. *Faith and History: A Comparison of Christian and Modern Views of History.* New York: Nord, 2013.

Nigosian, S. A. *World Faiths.* New York: St. Martin's, 1990.

Philo, *Questions and Answers on Genesis.* Translated by Ralph Marcus. Loeb Classical Library 380. Boston: Harvard University Press, 1953.

Pritchard, James B., ed. *The Ancient Near East: An Anthology of Texts & Pictures.* Princeton, NJ: Princeton University Press, 2011.

Provan, Iain. *A Serious Dangerous Religion: What the Old Testament Really Says and Why It Matters.* Waco, TX: Baylor, 2014.

Bibliography

Provan, Iain, et al. *A Biblical History of Israel.* Louisville: Westminster John Knox, 2003.

Thomas, W. H. Griffith, *The Holy Spirit of God.* Eugene, OR: Wipf & Stock, 2001.

von Rad, Gerhard. *Genesis: A Commentary.* Translated by John. H. Marks. Rev. ed. Old Testament Library. Philadelphia: Westminster, 1972.

———. *Old Testament Theology: The Theology of Israel's Historical Traditions.* Translated by D. M. G. Stalker. Louisville: Westminster John Knox, 1962.

Waltke, Bruce. *Genesis: A Commentary.* Grand Rapids: Zondervan, 2001.

Walton, John. *Genesis 1 as Ancient Cosmology.* Winona Lake, IN: Eisenbrauns, 2011.

Warren, Rick. Interview with *HuffPost.* https://www.youtube.com/watch?v=o3Z5C1nxCJI.

www.ingramcontent.com/pod-product-compliance
Lightning Source LLC
Chambersburg PA
CBHW050837160426
43192CB00011B/2057